DAINGEAN

1 7 APR 2021

WITHDRAWN

Crochet!

Crochet!

Techniques · Stitches · Patterns

by Marie-Noëlle Bayard

Photography by
Jean-Charles Vaillant

sixth&spring books
New York, NY

TABLE OF CONTENTS

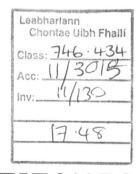
Leabharlann
Chontae Uíbh Fhailí

Class: 746·434
Acc: 11/3015
Inv: 11/130

17·48

Preface

Forget all the put-downs you've heard about crochet: It's old-hat, fuddy-duddy, outdated, out of style, or just plain ugly, as I've been told from time to time. With this book, I hope to show you otherwise. Crochet isn't just a limp, lace edging for tired-looking doilies or trimmings on granny dresses from generations ago.

Crochet is a fantastic technique, endlessly varied, which lets you fashion dramatic contrasts that look like complex weaves or spectacularly textured fabrics. Sure enough, a new wave of designers woke up to the beauty of hand-crafted fashions a few seasons back. Experienced needle-crafters could pick out, among the most sophisticated design collections, real masterpieces worked entirely in crochet: dresses, cover-ups, finishing touches for tailored outfits, overcoats, belts, carry-alls, and more. Whenever "hand made" makes yet another come-back, crochet is in the forefront because—in contrast to knitting or lace-making—no machine can reproduce the effect of hand-worked crochet. Crochet itself is a guarantee that real hand-crafts will always be sought after.

Join me on the road to discovery of *Crochet!* The hook—the only tool you need—is startlingly simple to use. With only a few twists of the wrist, it lets you into a vast treasury of pattern stitches. Learn the basics with the step-by-step instructions, and pick up lots of tips to make your work truly special. The more complicated pattern stitches are only slight variations on a few basic stitches. Techniques for increasing and decreasing allow you to lighten the fabric or make it denser. By working a few loops together, your crochet can expand to astonishing volumes. The work grows quickly, it's never boring, and in no time you'll find you have an absorbing new hobby.

Bringing crochet into today's world and adding new dimensions, there's an amazing variety of yarn fibers other than the traditional cotton, which still remains a marvelous fiber for making crochet lace. Follow my lead and throw yourself into the wide range of wools, including lambswool, mohair, cashmere, tweed, chenille, and more; silks, such as floss, high-sheen, raw silk; cottons, in perle, matte, and mercerised; and now new fibers such as bamboo and microfibers.

Play around with materials, colors, stitches. Everything is allowed! Crochet is a magnificent adventure that opens the doors to your wildest imagination and creativity.

Marie-Noëlle Bayard

1
TECHNIQUES

For good crochet technique, you need the right materials (hooks, yarn, etc.,) to achieve the proper result. Weight, texture, the composition of fibers, as well as the size of the hook, are fundamental to the effect you're aiming for. You'll acquire a whole vocabulary of terms, abbreviations, and symbols as you progress.

Although the learning curve may seem steep at first, you'll soon become familiar with crochet. Once you know the basics, you'll be able to judge how easy or challenging a pattern is, and make a plan to reach the desired result.

Yarns

There's a dazzling diversity of yarn fibers available for working with crochet. The look of the finished pattern depends on your choice of yarn fiber, texture, and color.

On the paper band around each ball of yarn you'll find an explanation of the contents. Keep a band with your work until you've completed the project. The band offers other useful information: the quality of the yarn, what it's made of, the weight of the ball or skein, the suggested hook size, the gauge or number of stitches and rows to the inch or centimeter, the color and batch number—an important number to know if you run out of yarn and need to find a perfect match to complete your project. When you mention the batch number to the yarn shop, you should be able to find more yarn from the batch that matches your initial purchase.

FIBERS OF ANIMAL ORIGIN

The same yarns are used for both crochet and knitting. You can easily find yarns at specialty boutiques, in mail-order catalogs, and on the Internet. Most yarns are shown in a range of colors developed by the manufacturers to reflect the trends for the season.

Lambswool

Made up of 100% long-staple wool fibers, lambs-wool yarn may carry the Woolmark label, which guarantees the quality of the yarn and states where it originated. Fine and tightly spun, this wool is well adapted to crochet and can be used to work many different stitches, whether new or classic.

Merino wool

Extremely soft and made up of long staple fibers, merino is very light, very warm, and somewhat elastic. These are the qualities that make merino particularly suitable for baby clothes or for elegant garments for women.

Tweed wool

From Scotland or Ireland, where the black-face Hebridean sheep flourish, tweed is strong and presents a sturdy appearance, in natural colors borrowed from plants native to the region.

Craftsmen use tweed yarn to weave the famous Harris tweed or to knit the Aran-pattern sweaters long favored by sailors. Some tweed wools have a slightly felted look; they are somewhat heavier and are worked with a 4 mm or 4.5 mm hook.

Baby wool

Soft as can be, this yarn is produced from the first shearing of lambs when they are 6 to 7 months old. The yarn may be pure wool or a mixture of wool and other fine fibers such as cashmere or alpaca. Baby wool is especially suitable for special items such as layettes.

Mohair

The mohair goat originated in Turkey. Mohair fibers are very long and foamy in texture, which lends mohair an appearance resembling sheep's wool. The description "kid mohair" means that the fiber was obtained from a shearing of very young animals.

Alpaca

This fiber is obtained from a domesticated cousin of the camel that is native to South America. The fiber is soft, fine, smooth, and slightly elastic. Alpaca may be pure or mixed with sheep's wool. Because each alpaca yields only 4 to 6 lbs (2–3 kg) of fleece a year, alpaca is usually kept for classic or unusual patterns.

Cashmere

The cashmere goat originated in the high valleys of the Himalayas. The fleece is made up of long, fine hair and a downy undercoat. Only the undercoat is used for cashmere yarn, which is why the yarn has a silky, light, and elastic appearance and feel. Because the cashmere goat does not secrete lanolin, it cannot be sheared. Instead, each animal is combed once each year in the spring time, which results in a yield of about 3 to 5 ounces (100–150 g) per animal. 100% cashmere fiber is rarely on the market; most cashmere yarns contain at least 25% wool fibers.

For crochet, very high-pile yarns such as angora are not generally used, because the stitches disappear among the fibers and it is extremely difficult to obtain an even finish.

Silk

The mulberry silk moth, or *Bombyx mori*, in its larval form secretes this extremely soft fiber, which has exceptional thermal qualities. The cocoon that surrounds the chrysalis is made up of a single thread between 1000 and 1500 yards (700 to 1200 meters) long. The cocoons are subjected to a steaming process to harvest the fiber. Thanks to its chemical composition, silk readily takes dye. Silk yarn for crochet or knitting comes in a wide range of colors.

FIBERS OF PLANT ORIGIN

Among the plant fiber family, cotton yarn stands out for its strength, the quality of its staple, its texture, and a huge range of deep dyed colors, which tells you that the yarn won't fade even if washed in hot water (140–195 degrees Fahrenheit [60–90 degrees centigrade]). Cotton is widely used for decorative items and, especially, for crochet lace.

Mercerized cotton

Cotton threads for crochet are often mercerized: they are treated with chemicals to give them a high sheen and make the fibers firmer. Mercerized cotton is usually a fine thread made up of 2 twisted strands; it is worked with a 2 mm or 2.5 mm hook.

Fil d'Ecosse

Also known as lisle thread, fil d'Ecosse (Scottish yarn) is spun from the finest, long-staple Egyptian cotton. It also undergoes mercerisation. Fil d'Ecosse is spun from 4 tightly twisted strands, which give a firm finish and a slightly corded surface.

Matte cotton twist

Matte cotton has a more rustic, nonshiny finish because it is not subjected to mercerization. Less tightly spun the preceding yarns, matte cotton seems more fragile but is very supple to the touch when it is worked into crochet.

Perle cotton

Perle cotton is composed of two very tightly spun strands, which results in a raised, cabled effect. Having a glossy finish, perle cotton is widely used for embroidery, as well as for decorative crochet items.

Viscose

Viscose rayon fiber is derived from a number of natural sources, including wood, bamboo, and soy. It is very supple and shiny. The feel is reminiscent of silk. Crochet lends body to viscose.

Linen

Linen fiber is obtained from the stems of linen flax. Like linen fabrics, linen yarn for knitting or crochet is soft, supple, light, and comfortable to wear. It is available in the form of matte-finish, loosely twis-ted strands and is suitable for working with a 3.5 mm or 4 mm crochet hook. Very fine linen threads are used for making the finest lace.

SYNTHETIC YARNS

Sometimes blended with natural fibers, synthetic materials offer contrasting qualities of beauty and utility. All manner of fantasy effects are possible with polyesters, polyamides, acrylics, microfibers, metallic yarns, Lurex, and more. Most have good thermal qualities and high resistance to wear, which allows machine washing. However, crochet with synthetics can require special care, because yarns that are too "hairy" or plush conceal the structure of the preceding row and make it difficult to place the hook in the right place. We strongly advise making a sample swatch before embarking on a project with yarns of these kinds.

UNUSUAL YARNS

You can use almost any material when working with crochet. The one essential: The fiber must be in the form of a yarn or narrow strips. Everything goes: ribbon, leather laces, electric wire, fine brass wire, magnetic tape, plastic cords, and more. It's often fun to find out what you can do with unusual resources, but technical problems sometimes arise in the course of the work because of unforeseen characteristics inherent in the materials.

Tools

The only tool you need for crochet is a hook. Use it for pattern stitches, finishing borders, and sometimes for joining up the parts of a pattern.

HOOKS

Hooks come in different sizes. Choose your hook according to the thickness and type of yarn you're going to work with. The number engraved on the hook is its diameter in millimeters and is the same as the size shown on knitting needles. The appropriate hook size is always indicated on the paper wrapping for balls or skeins of yarn. You'll find a range of hooks in different sizes and a variety of materials at notions counters, yarn shops, and specialty boutiques.

Metal hooks are available in a large range of sizes. Metal is a strong and resistant material that doesn't get bent out of shape and lets the stitches glide smoothly. Metal crochet hooks are perfect for beginners, who can expect to keep their hooks for a long time. Most hooks have a flattened section that makes it easy to hold your thumb and index finger in the right position. Some metal hooks also have a plastic sheath, which makes it easier to grasp the tool. The finest metal hooks are suitable for lace work. Bamboo hooks have a very smooth surface and are pleasant to use. They are available in sizes 2.5 mm to 10 mm or 12 mm and are suitable for use with cotton or woolen yarns.

Plastic hooks are less sturdy and may twist or break when used with strong or stiff yarns. They are best used with thick, supple twists. Plastic hooks are not recommended for crafters who tend to work very tightly, because the plastic point will not easily go through the stitches of preceding rows.

Most of the hooks on the market are labeled with the metric system. However, a few outlets sell hooks—especially steel hooks—with numbers corresponding to the English/USA systems. The table on page 14 will help you identify the hooks you need.

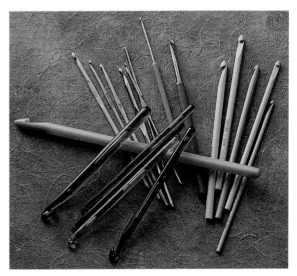

DRESSMAKING TOOLS

When working with crochet, you'll need a few other tools within reach:

• A tape measure to measure your sample swatches and to keep track of the progress of your project

• A darning or tapestry needle for joining the seams of the various sections of your pattern

• Row counter to keep track of the number of rows or repeats of a complicated pattern stitch

• Scissors for cutting threads

• A notebook and a pencil to note the number of rows and stitches in a sample swatch, as well as notes you need to jot down in the course of working a pattern.

MATCHING HOOKS

Metric system (France) (mm)	U.K. (No.)	U.S. (No.)	Materials
0.6	25-26		Metal
0.75	23-24		Metal
1.0	21-22		Metal
1.25	19-20		Metal
1.5	17-18		Metal
1.75	15-16		Metal
2.0	14	14	Metal or bamboo
	13	13	
2.5	12	12	Metal or bamboo
3.0	11	11	Metal or bamboo
	10	10	
3.5	9	9	Metal or bamboo
4.0	8	8	Metal or bamboo
4.5	7	7	Metal or bamboo
5.0	6	6	Metal or bamboo
5.5	5	5	Metal or plastic
6	4	4	Plastic
6.5			Plastic
7	2	3	Plastic
8		2	Plastic
9		1	Plastic
10		0	Metal or Plastic
12		00	Metal or Plastic
15			Metal or Plastic
16			Plastic

Instructions, abbreviations, and symbols

The text accompanying the patterns is written in abbreviations, and the charts are put together with symbols. Here's a summary of components that appear at the start of a pattern, followed by a few tips.

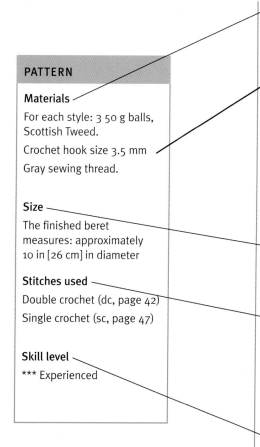

PATTERN

Materials
For each style: 3 50 g balls, Scottish Tweed.
Crochet hook size 3.5 mm
Gray sewing thread.

Size
The finished beret measures: approximately 10 in [26 cm] in diameter

Stitches used
Double crochet (dc, page 42)
Single crochet (sc, page 47)

Skill level
*** Experienced

TIP

Remember: Crochet technique demands patience. It's important to follow the instructions step by step in the course of working the pattern.

- **Materials:** This section indicates the type of yarn you'll need, as well as the size of hook recommended to complete the pattern.

- **Crochet hook size:** If you use a size different from the one recommended, pick a hook one half-size larger or smaller than the size indicated in the pattern. For example: If the pattern advises a hook size 3.5 mm and you tend to work tightly, choose a size 4 mm. On the other hand, if your work tends to be loose, pick a size 3 mm.

- **The size of the finished work or the garment size:** Make sure that the size matches the one you intend.

- **Stitches used:** The list of stitches gives you an opportunity to judge how difficult the pattern is likely to be. If you've never mastered the proposed stitch, try it out in a sample swatch before you start work on the pattern.

- **Skill level:** The number of stars indicates the degree of difficulty.

* not difficult, suitable for beginners.

** pattern requires some familiarity with crochet technique.

*** pattern recommended for experts.

ABBREVIATIONS

You will find the following common abbreviations in most crochet patterns. Abbreviations of stitches appear in another table.

ch	chain
cont	continue
dec	decrease
foll	following
inc	increase
lp	loop
r	row
rep	repeat
rnd	round
st	stitch
tog	together

ASTERISKS

When you see the asterisk * symbol, you know you need to repeat a stitch or section. Over one row, a pattern repeat appears between two asterisks, as follows: * 2 ch sts, skip 1 st, work 2 dc in foll st *. Repeat from * to * across the row. It's essential to repeat the identical series of stitches very precisely to keep your pattern and texture regular. Usually, the beginning and end of the row are outside the repeat sequence and the appropriate instructions are given before and after the asterisks.

PARENTHESES

Instructions enclosed in parentheses must be worked in the order given and repeated according to the instructions following the closing parenthesis. For example: Work (2 ch sts, 3 dc in foll dc) 3 times. The words in parentheses may be either different parts of the same pattern stitch or the detail of a pattern that must be repeated a certain number of times.

YOUR SAMPLE SWATCH

Every craftsperson has his or her own style of crochet ... a little tighter, a little looser. At times, these differences can result in a considerable size difference between the finished work and the indicated measurements. That's why it's essential to complete a sample swatch before you embark on a pattern.

Using the same yarn and crochet hook as specified for the pattern, work a sample swatch 4 in [10 cm] square. Place the swatch flat (press it lightly, if necessary) and check that the overall size, as well as the stitch count and the number of rows matches the dimensions given.

To check the number of stitches, place 2 pins upright 2 in [5 cm] apart across the width and count the stitches in between. To check the number of rows, place 2 pins upright 2 in [5 cm] apart along the length and count the rows between them. If the sample swatch has fewer stitches and rows than the pattern advises, your work is too slack. Use a smaller crochet hook. If the sample swatch has more stitches and rows than the pattern advises, your work is too tight. Use a larger crochet hook.

Symbols	Abbreviations/Instructions
○	**chain stitch (ch st) or ch**
●	**slip stitch (sl st):** insert hook in a st, draw lp up and through st on hook
┼	**single crochet (sc; UK: double crochet, dc):** insert hook in a st, draw up lp, yo and draw lp through the 2 remaining lps on the hook
┬	**+ or X half-double crochet (half dc; UK: half-tr):** yo, insert hook in a st, draw up lp, yo and draw lp through the 3 remaining lps on hook
┬̄	**double crochet (dc; UK: treble crochet, tr):** yo, insert hook in a st, draw up lp, yo and draw lp through first 2 lps on hook, yo and draw lp through remaining 2 lps on hook
┬̿	**treble crochet (tr; UK: dbl tr):** yo twice, insert hook in a st, draw up lp, yo and draw lp through 2 lps on hook, yo and draw lp through 2 lps on hook, yo and draw lp through remaining 2 lps on hook
┬̄̿	**double treble crochet (dbl tr; UK, triple treble, tr tr):** yo 3 times, insert hook in a st, draw up lp, * yo and draw lp through 2 lps on hook *, rep from * to * twice, yo and draw lp through remaining 2 lps on hook

Symbols	Abbreviations/Instructions
∓	**triple treble (tr tr; UK quadruple tr, quad tr):** yo 4 times, insert hook in a st, draw up 1 lp, * yo and draw lp through 2 lps on hook *, rep from * to * 3 times, yo and draw lp through remaining 2 lps on hook
ʃ	**raised dc worked from front (raised dcf):** yo, insert hook sideways from front to back, right to left, around the stem of the dc in the preceding row, draw up a lp, yo and draw lp through 2 lps on hook, yo and draw lp through remaining 2 lps on hook
ʃ	**raised dc worked from back (raised dcb):** yo, insert hook sideways from back to front, right to left, around the stem of the dc in the preceding row, draw up a lp, yo and draw lp through 2 lps on hook, yo and draw lpthrough remaining 2 lps on hook
ʃ	**raised treble worked from front (raised trf):** yo twice, insert hook sideways from front to back, right to left, around the stem of the dc in the preceding row, draw up a lp, yo and draw lp through 2 lps on hook, yo and draw lp through next 2 lps on hook, yo and draw lp through remaining 2 lps on hook
ʃ	**raised treble worked from back (raised trb):** yo twice, insert hook sideways from front to back, right to left, around the stem of the dc in the preceding row, draw up a lp, yo and draw lp through 2 lps on hook, yo and draw lp through next 2 lps on hook, yo and draw lp through remaining 2 lps on hook
A	**2 dc tog (UK: 2 tr tog):** * yo, insert hook in a st, draw up lp, yo and draw lp through 2 lps on hook *, rep from * to * once, then working over foll st, yo, draw lp through the remaining 3 lps on hook
A	**3 dc tog (UK: 3 tr tog):** * yo, insert hook in a st, draw up lp, yo and draw lp through 2 lps on hook *, rep from * to * twice, then working over foll sts, yo, draw lp through the remaining 4 lps on hook
	3 tr tog (UK: 3 dbl tr tog): * yo twice, insert hook in a st, draw up lp, (yo and draw

Symbols	Abbreviations/Instructions
	lp through 2 lps on hook) twice *, working into foll 3 sts rep from * to * 3 times , then yo and draw lp through remaining 4 lps on hook
	3 dbl tr tog (UK: 3 tr tr tog): * yo 3 times, insert hook in a st, draw up lp, yo and draw lp through 2 lps on hook, yo and draw lp through 2 lps on hook, yo and draw lp through 2 lps on hook *, rep from * to * twice, inserting hook in foll 2 sts, then yo and draw lp through remaining 4 lps on hook
	4 dbl tr tog (UK: 4 tr tr tog): * yo 4 times, insert hook in a st, draw up lp, yo and draw lp through 2 lps on hook *, rep from * to * times, inserting hook in foll 3 sts, then yo and draw lp through the remaining 5 lps on hook
	Crossed double crochets (crossed dc; UK: crossed tr): yo twice, insert hook in a st, draw up lp, yo and draw lp through 2 lps, leaving remaining 3 lps on hook; yo, skip a st, insert hook in foll st, draw up a lp, yo and draw lp through 2 lps on hook, yo and draw lp through 2 lps on hook = 3 lps on hook. Now yo and draw lp through 2 loops on hook, yo, and draw lp through 2 lps on hook = 1 st on hook. Finally, work 1 ch st, yo insert hook under both upper strands where preceding dc crosses over, draw up a lp, yo and draw lp through 2 lps, yo and draw lp through remaining 2 lps.
	Granular sc (gsc): Work this stitch on the ws. Insert hook in next st, yo and draw up lp, (yo and work 1 st off hook) 3 times, thus working 3 ch sts; yo and slip off remaining 2 lps; pull each "grain" to rs of work.
	Group of petals (gp): Work (1 sc, 1 half-dc, 3 dc) around the stem of the indicated stitch
	triangular bar (tb): Work 6 ch, 1 sc in 2nd ch st from hook, 1 tr in foll ch st, 1 dc in next ch st, 1 tr in foll ch st, 1 dbl tr in foll st

Symbols	Abbreviations/Instructions
	rosette: Work (1 dc, 2 ch) 9 times into the same st, slightly extend the loop on the hook and withdraw the hook then reinsert it from ws to rs through the top of the first dc of rosette, keeping the sts at the back of the work. Pick up the dropped st and draw it through the lp on the hook.
	Cluster stitch (formed of 3 dc): A cluster st may be formed of almost any number of sts; the number is always specified in the instructions for the pattern stitch and is indicated in the symbol. * yo, insert hook in a st, draw up lp, yo, draw lp through 2 loops on hook *, rep from * to * twice, working into the same st of the previous rnd or row. Now yo and draw lp through remaining 4 st on hook.
	Puff st (formed of half tr): A puff st may be formed of almost any number of sts; the number is always specified in the instructions for the pattern stitch and is indicated in the symbol). * yo, insert hook in first ch st, yo and draw out the loop (you will end up with 3 loops on the hook) *, rep from * to * twice, working into same st of previous rnd or row; yo and pull the hook through all 7 lps on hook, then work 1 sl st to hold the puff st in place.
	Bobble (formed of 5 dc) A bobble may be formed of almost any number of sts; the number is always specified in the instructions for the pattern stitch and is indicated by the symbol). Work the group of dc, usually 5, into a single st of the previous row or rnd; to bring the st into relief, withdraw the hook from the last st worked, reinsert it through the top of the first of the 5 just worked and pull loop through the top of the dc on the hook. Push the puffed part of the bobble through to the rs of the work.
	Picot formed of 3 sts (picot is worked with several chain sts; the exact number is always specified in the instructions for the stitch) 1 sc, work 3 ch, 1 sl st through the first of the 3 ch.

Symbols	Abbreviations/Instructions
	Diagonal elongated double crochet (dedc): yo, insert hook in same st and first st in preceding group of 3 dc, yo and draw up lp, extending it to the height of the row of dc you are working (yo and work 2 lps off hook) twice.
	Crab stitch (single crochet [sc] from left to right): In the final row, do not turn the work but instead insert the hook from front to back and left to right; draw up a lp, turning the hook up, yo and draw through the lp to complete the sc, insert hook in foll st from left to right to form the second st.
	Shell stitch: Skip 4 sts, work 6 tr, inserting the hook from right to left under the next dc and working over the length of this dc; now work 6 dc, inserting the hook from left to right under the next dc and working back over the length of this dc; skip 4 dc.
	Bundle: (yo, insert hook, yo and draw up a lp, slightly extend this last lp) into each of the sts specified in the instructions. Yo, draw through all the loops on the hook, then work 1 ch st to hold the bundle firmly.

Getting started

HOW TO HOLD THE YARN AND THE HOOK

IF YOU'RE RIGHT-HANDED

1. Hold the hook in your right hand as if it were a pencil, with the hook end pointing downward and the thumb and index finger on either side of the flattened section.

2. Take the yarn in your left hand and, to maintain the tension, thread it between your little and index fingers.

NOTE

The instructions in this book are written for right-handed crocheters. If you're a leftie, place a mirror next to the photos that show you how to work the stitches. This will let you picture the correct way to hold the hook and yarn as you follow the instructions.

IF YOU'RE LEFT-HANDED

1. Hold the hook in your left hand as if it were a pencil, with the hook end pointing downward and the thumb and index finger on either side of the flattened section.

2. Take the yarn in your right hand and, to maintain the tension, thread it between your little and index fingers.

WORKING YOUR FIRST STITCH

1. Form a loop around the base of your thumb.

2. Insert the end of the hook into the loop.

3–4. Bring the yarn over by pulling the yarn from the ball over the hook.

5. Draw the yarn from the ball through this loop.

6. Gently close the loop over the hook.

7. Place the knot in position under the hook.

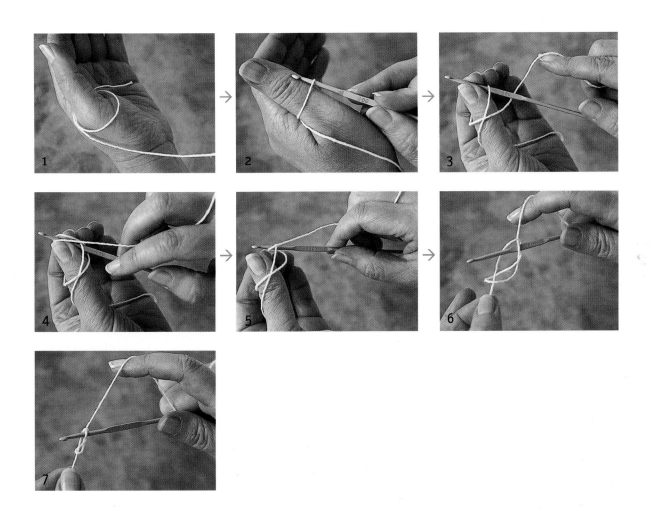

CHAIN STITCH

1. Work the first stitch, then pass the yarn that comes from the ball over the hook= 1 yo.

2. Pull the hook from left to right to draw the yo through the loop, gently pull on the loop.

3. To work a chain, yo, pull the hook from left to right to draw the yo through the loop on the hook, and so on.

4. You will end up with a base chain made up of chain stitches.

CHANGING THE YARN

STOPPING THE WORK

To stop the work at end of the last row, work 1 ch st, cut the yarn leaving a length of about 4 in [10 cm]. Thread the yarn end through the chain st and pull gently to close. Using a darning or tapestry needle, darn the yarn end through the edge sts.

1. To change colors or join the yarn from a new ball, begin the stitch with the yarn you're working with.

2. While working the final yo of the st you're working on, work in the new strand. Complete the stitch.

3. Begin the stitch with the first yarn and complete it with the second, leaving a length of about 4 in [10 cm] for each strand.

4. Once you have completed the work, darn the thread end on ws of work using a darning or tapestry needle.

INCREASING

You may increase at the beginning, in the middle, or at the end of a row, creating a different effect according to where you increased.

AT THE BEGINNING OF A ROW, INCREASE BY 1 SINGLE STITCH

Work this increase at beginning of row, working twice into the first stitch, no matter what pattern you're working on. The examples we show are all in single crochet.

1. Work 1 ch to turn.

2. Work 1 sc in following st.

3. Work a 2nd sc in the same stitch.

4–5. Cont as indicated.

ADD SEVERAL STITCHES AT END OF ROW

1. At end of row, work as many ch sts as you need to add stitches.

2. Turn the work.

3. Continue as follows: Work 1 ch to turn, skip first ch st and cont working sc over the chain you added.

4. Continue as indicated.

ADD ONE OR MORE STITCHES
WHILE WORKING A ROW OR ROUND

While working the pattern, increase 1 st by working twice into same st. If you work into the same st 3 times, you will increase by 2 stitches. Continuing in this way, you can increase by as many stitches as you need.

1. Beg by working sc.

2. Next, where indicated in the instructions, work 1 or 2 supplementary stitches by working 2 or 3 times into the same stitch.

3. Work sc to end of row.

This way of increasing with several stitches at the edge, unlike some other methods, avoids forming "stair steps".

DECREASE SEVERAL STITCHES AT BEGINNING OF ROW

There are several ways to decrease, just as there are several ways to increase. The easiest way to decrease at the end of a row is not to work over the stitches in the previous row, leaving the number of stitches indicated for decreasing in the instructions or chart. The samples shown in the photos were worked in double crochets.

DECREASE BY ONE STITCH

To decrease by 1 dc, 1 st from the edge, work 3 ch to count as first dc of row or rnd.

2–3: * yo, insert hook in a st, draw up a lp, yo and draw lp through 2 lps on hook* .

4. Rep from * to * twice more.

5. yo and draw lp through 3 loops on hook.

6. Cont the row in double crochets.

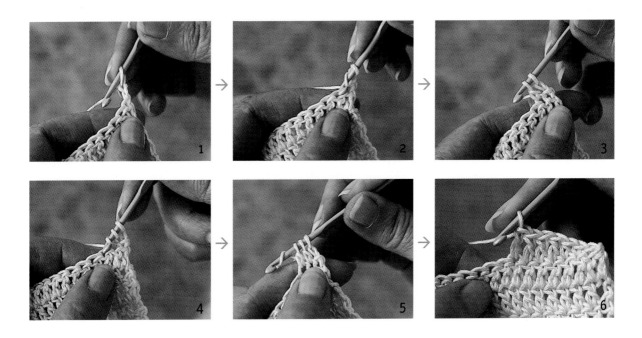

DECREASE BY SEVERAL STITCHES

To form a rounded section, progressively change the height of the stitches as you work.

1. Beg decreasing with sl sts, then work in sc.

2. Switch to half-dc, then dc.

This type of decrease is recommended for armholes and necklines, where it's important to avoid a stair-step effect.

DECREASE AT END OF ROW

DECREASE BY 1 DC, 1 ST FROM THE EDGE

1. When 3 dc remain from the preceding round, continue as follows: work 1 dc in next-to-last st.

2. Skip the next st and work 1 dc in foll st.

3. Now work 1 tr in last st of row.

DECREASE BY SEVERAL DC

1. At beg of next row, work sl sts over the sts in the preceding row to return to the level where the work continues.

2. To start the next section, work as many chain sts as necessary to match the height of the stitches in the row (for example, 3 ch correspond to 1 dc; 2 ch correspond to 1 half-dc; 1 ch corresponds to 1 sc).

3. Work over the number of stitches to decrease as at the beginning of the row, but in reverse order. Make the stitches progressively taller to form a rounded section. Begin by working 1 dc, continue with 1 half-dc over the second-to-last stitch, and end by working 1 single crochet over the last stitch in the row.

ARMHOLES

Armholes can be worked in three different ways to match the shoulder cap of the sleeve.

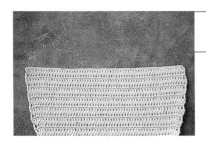

SQUARE ARMHOLE

This is the simplest armhole shape. In a single row, fasten off the number of stitches corresponding to the top of the sleeves and part of the sides of the garment.

CLASSIC ARMHOLE

Form the classic armhole by progressively decreasing the number of stitches on the sides of the garment until you have reached the desired shoulder width. Shape the shoulder cap row by row to match the armhole, so that both sections are the same length. The shoulder cap will fit easily into the armhole.

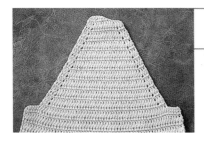

RAGLAN ARMHOLE

In the raglan armhole, the shoulder cap reaches all the way to the neck. The decreases are worked progressively from the underarm to the neckline, skipping 1 to 3 stitches on the edges to avoid forming the stair-step effect. The shoulder caps are worked to match in the same way. The top of the sleeve forms part of the neckline. At the top of the sleeve, leave a width of 3 to 6 in [7 to 15 cm], depending on the depth of the neckline.

NECKLINES

There are three basic neckline shapes, just as there are three ways to work the armholes.

SQUARE NECK

This is the simplest neckline. The first decrease is worked between 2 and 6 in [5 and 15 cm] from the top of the shoulder. To shape the square neck, stop working over the indicated number of center stitches and complete the 2 sides separately as far as the shoulders.

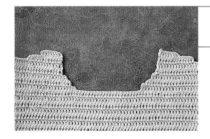

ROUND OR CREW NECK

Begin the round neck 2 in [5 cm] below the shoulder line. Stop working over the indicated number of center stitches; this number is generally one-third of the total number of stitches to be decreased. Complete the 2 sides separately to complete the shoulders, decreasing progressively row by row at the neck edge, until you have formed the neckline desired.

After you have joined up the front and back of the garment, work 2 rows of single crochet (or whichever stitch is given in the pattern) to cover up the stair-step effect caused by the neckline decreases.

V NECK

Begin the V-neck between 6 and 10 in [15 and 25 cm] below the shoulder line, or just after beginning the armhole decreases. Divide the work into equal sections. At the neck edge, decrease progressively by slipping 1 to 3 stitches. This type of neckline does not usually need a finishing border, unless the pattern indicates a special edging.

33

BUTTONHOLES

Buttonholes can be worked in various ways, according to the desired effect. Here are the three buttonholes most often used. The examples are worked in single crochet, but the technique is the same no matter what stitch is used.

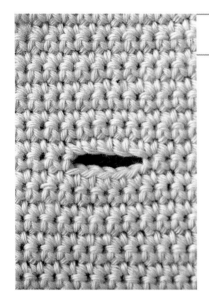

HORIZONTAL BUTTONHOLE

In the first row, work as far as the buttonhole position, skip the number of stitches corresponding to the diameter of the button and work the equivalent number of chain stitches (e.g., skip 5, ch 5) then continue the row beginning in the following st. Next row: Simply work the regular pattern stitches (in this case, single crochets) over the chain stitches.

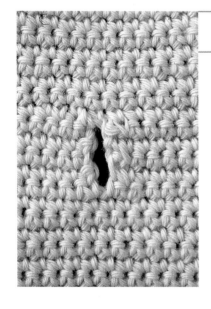

VERTICAL BUTTONHOLE

With rs of work facing, work as far as the buttonhole position. Turn the work with ws facing and work back and forth until the number of short rows corresponds to the diameter of the button, ending with a right-side row; leave this work aside. Rejoin the yarn with a sl st in the st following the one where you made the first turn. Work the same number of rows back and forth, ending with a wrong-side row. Next row: Pick up the yarn left aside to cont across the entire row and complete the pattern.

LOOP BUTTONHOLE

While working the last row of the section or during the edging row, at the buttonhole position, skip the number of stitches corresponding to the button diameter and work the same number of chain stitches. Turn the work so that the chain is doubled back and work 1 sl st into the last sc. Now continue over the chain with the same number of sc as ch sts. Note that the chain must be completely covered: if you have too few stitches, the chain will show through; if you have too many stitches, the buttonhole loop will warp. Complete the loop by working a sl st over the next st and complete the final or edging row in pattern stitch.

PUTTING IT ALL TOGETHER

HIDING THE LOOSE ENDS

Before you join up the various sections of a garment, it's important to hide all the loose ends of yarn. With wrong side of work facing, use a darning or tapestry needle to weave the loose end into the crochet stitches for a length of at least 2 in [5 cm]. Trim the end even with the surface of the crochet.

JOINING WITH THE CROCHET HOOK

1. Place the 2 sections right sides together and pin or tack to hold them in place stitch by stitch.

2. Insert the hook through the upper strand only of the first stitch in each section.

3. Draw up a loop and work 1 chain stitch.

* Insert the hook through the upper strand of the next stitch on the edge of both pieces, draw up a loop, yarn over, and draw the hook through both loops (= 1 single crochet). Continue from * until you have completed the seam. Fasten off. Repeat until all the sections are joined.

JOINING BY NEEDLE WITH A BACKSTITCH SEAM

Place the 2 sections' right sides together and pin or tack to hold them in place stitch by stitch. Use a darning or tapestry needle to work backstitch from right to left 1 complete stitch from the edge and through both thicknesses of fabric. Work backstitch as follows:

1. Insert needle straight through fabric from top to bottom layer, reinsert needle in bottom layer 2 stitches ahead and bring it through the top layer.

2–3. Insert needle at end of previous stitch and repeat, working each stitch from halfway through the previous one. This type of stitching results in a very firm join that can be a little bulky along the seamline.

JOINING BY OVERCASTING WITH A NEEDLE

Place the 2 sections' right sides together, making sure the edges are even, and pin or tack to hold them in place stitch by stitch.

1–3. Working from left to right, overcast the matching stitches in both sections, making sure that you work through the full thicknesses. Overcasting results in a less neat finish than backstitching, but the seam is also less bulky.

2

BASICS

These stitches are the fundamentals of crochet. They are used to form every pattern stitch in an infinite variety. These basics are shown in order of complexity, from the simplest chain stitch to the more involved double crochet. You can combine basic stitches to create a fabric that is more or less open and airy. As soon as a crochet novice learns to control the yarn tension, any pattern is within reach.

Basic stitches

SINGLE CROCHET

NOTE

For the first row of all the basic stitches, start with a base chain of chain stitches.

1. Insert hook into 2nd stitch from hook.

2. Yarn over.

3. Draw the loop through the stitch.

4. Yarn over.

5. Draw the yarn through 2 loops on hook. On completing each row, work 1 ch st to turn.

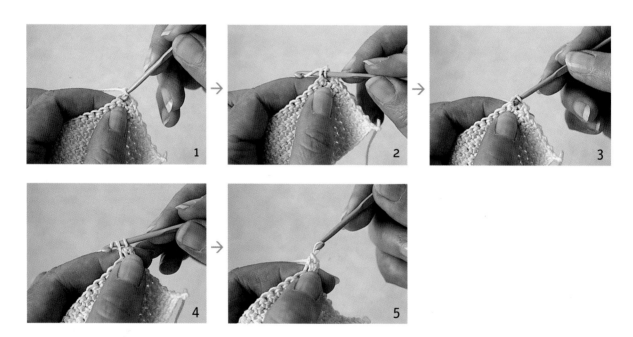

SLIP STITCH

1. Insert hook into 2nd stitch from hook.

2. * Yarn over.

3. Draw the yarn through the stitch and loop. Repeat from * to work the next slip stitch.

HALF-DOUBLE CROCHET

1. Yarn over.

2. Insert hook in 3rd stitch from hook.

3. Yarn over.

4. Draw the yarn through the stitch.

5. Yarn over.

6. Draw the loop through all 3 loops on hook. On completing each row work 2 chain stitches to turn.

 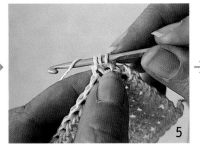 

DOUBLE CROCHET

1. Yarn over.

2. Insert hook in 4th stitch from hook. Yarn over.

3. Draw the yarn through the stitch and again yarn over.

4. Draw the yarn through the first 2 loops on hook.

5. Yarn over.

6–7. Draw the yarn through the remaining 2 loops. On completing each row, work 3 ch to turn.

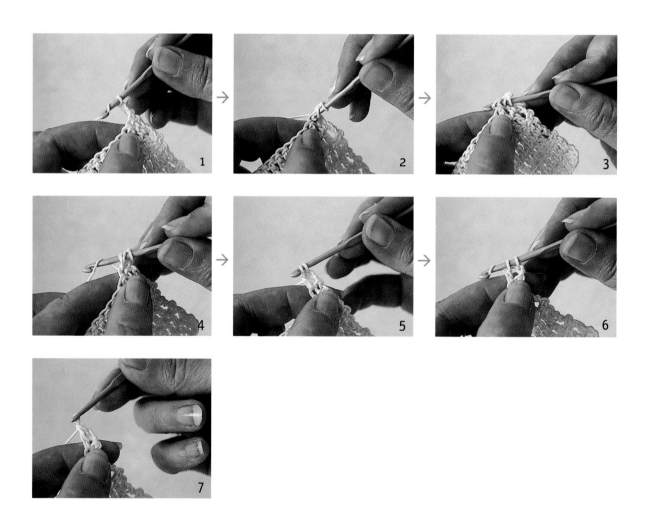

TREBLE CROCHET

1. Yarn over twice.

2. Insert hook in 5th stitch from hook. Yarn over.

3. Draw the yarn through the stitch.

4. Yarn over.

5. Draw the yarn through the first 2 loops on hook, yarn over.

6. Draw the yarn through the first 2 loops on hook, yarn over.

7. Draw the yarn through the remaining 2 loops. On completing each row, work 4 ch to turn.

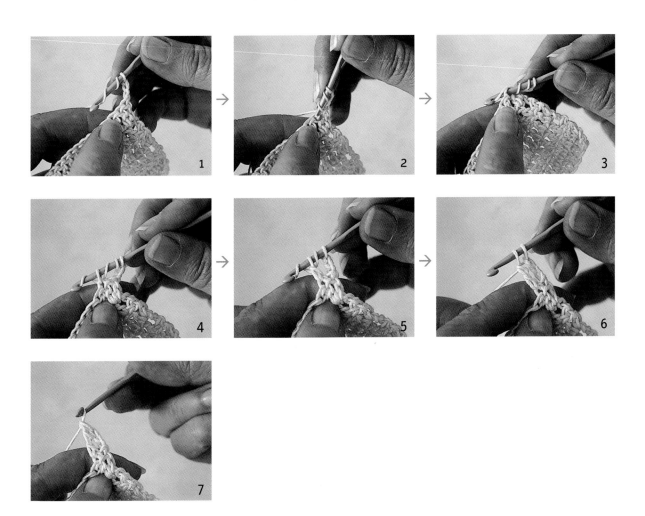

DOUBLE TREBLE CROCHET

1. Yarn over 3 times.

2. Insert hook in 6th stitch from hook. Yarn over.

3. Draw the yarn through the stitch.

4. Yarn over.

5. Draw the yarn through the first 2 loops on hook, yarn over.

6. Draw the yarn through the first 2 loops on hook, yarn over.

7. Draw the yarn through the first 2 loops on hook, yarn over.

8. Draw the yarn through the remaining 2 loops. On completing each row, work 5 ch to turn.

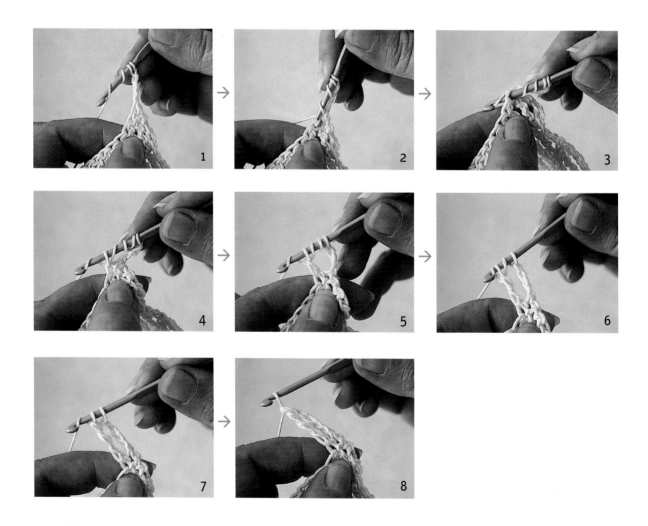

CRAB STITCH

This stitch is used to decorate or reinforce the edge of a crocheted item by forming a raised border. It is worked as for single crochet but in the opposite direction; that is, from left to right (for right-handed crocheters; the opposite for lefties).

1. On completing the row, do not turn the work. Insert the hook from front to back through the preceding stitch on the right.

2. With hook end turned down, pull 1 loop through the preceding row.

3. Yarn over.

4. Pull the loop through all the loops on the hook to complete the single crochet.

5. Insert the hook in the next stitch to the right to work another crab stitch. Working from left to right causes the yarn to twist, which lends a raised effect to the crab stitch.

WORKING IN ROWS

NOTE

It is necessary to work a number of chain stitches at the beginning of each row or round to bring your work to the level required for the stitches. The chain stitches at the beginning are equivalent to the height of the pattern stitch and count as the first stitch of the row.

Single crochet: Turn the work, 1 ch, insert hook in 2nd st from edge.

Half-double crochet: Turn the work, 2 ch, insert hook in 2nd stitch from edge.

Double crochet: Turn the work, 3 ch, insert hook in 2nd stitch from edge.

Treble crochet: Turn the work, 4 ch, insert hook in 2nd stitch from edge.

Double treble crochet: Turn the work, 5 ch, insert hook in 2nd stitch from edge.

Working in rows means just that: back and forth. Begin by working chain stitches for a base chain, according to the pattern instructions, or according to how many stitches you need for the width you require.

Row 1: At the beginning of the row, the instructions will tell you how many extra chain stitches to work. These extra chain stitches will stand upright alongside the basic pattern stitch used for the rest of the row. As you work Row 1, make sure that you insert your hook under the 2 or 3 strands that make up each stitch of the base chain.

Following rows: At the end of each row, turn the work to continue with the next row. Work as many chain stitches as necessary to reach the height of the basic pattern stitch (see note) and count these chain stitches as the first basic pattern stitch of the row. Insert the hook under both upper strands of the stitches in the preceding row.

Complete the row by working the last stitch over the final chain stitch at the beginning of the previous row.

Pattern stitches

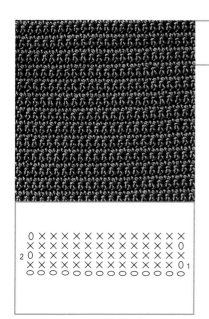

SINGLE CROCHET

This stitch is sometimes referred to as "rose stitch."

Work a base chain with as many chain stitches as you need for the width.

Row 1: 1 ch, skip 1st ch st of base chain, work 1 sc in foll st. Cont in sc across the row.

Row 2: 1 ch (to count as first sc), skip 1 st, 1 sc in foll st. Cont in sc across the row.

Following rows: Repeat Row 2.

RIBBED SINGLE CROCHET

Work a base chain with as many chain stitches as you need for the width.

Row 1: 1 ch, skip 1st ch st of base chain, work 1 sc in foll st. Cont in sc across the row.

Row 2: 1 ch (to count as first sc), skip 1 st, working under back strand only of st in preceding row, 1 sc in foll st. Cont working sc through back strand only across the row.

Following rows: Repeat Row 2.

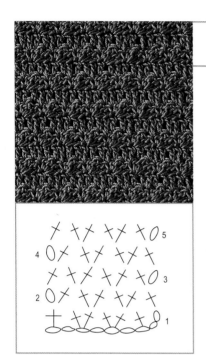

EYELET STITCH

Work chain stitches for a base chain in a multiple of 2 stitches plus 1 stitch.

Row 1: Skip 2 stitches, work 1 sc into the foll st, skip 1 ch st, * 2 sc into foll ch st, skip 1 ch st *, repeat from * to * across the row. End by working 1 sc in last ch st. Turn the work.

Row 2: 1 ch (to count as first sc of row), work 1 sc in first sc of preceding row, skip 1 sc, then work * 2 sc in next sc, skip 1 sc *, repeat from * to * across the row. End by working 1 sc in ch st of previous row.

Following rows: Repeat Row 2.

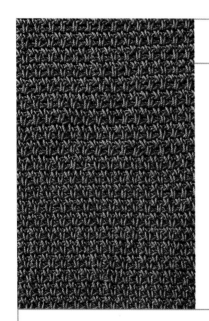

TIGHT GRANITE STITCH

Work chain stitches for a base chain in a multiple of 2.

Row 1: 1 ch, skip the first ch st, now work * 1 sc, 1 ch, skip 1 ch st *, repeat from * to * across the row. End by working 1 sc over the last ch st.

Row 2: 1 ch, skip 1st ch st, now work * 1 sc over ch st of previous row, 1 ch, skip 1 sc *, repeat from * to * across the row. End by working 1 sc over the 1st ch st of previous row.

Following rows: Repeat Row 2.

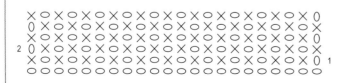

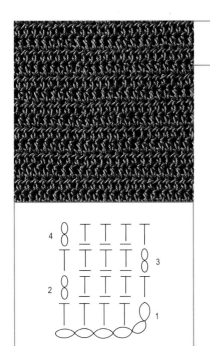

RIBBED HALF-DOUBLE CROCHET

Work a base chain with as many chain stitches as you need for the width.

Row 1: 2 ch (to count as first half-dc of row), skip 1 ch st, * work 1 half-dc in following stitch. Repeat from * across the row.

Row 2: 2 ch (= 1 half-dc), * skip 1 st, working under back strand only of st in previous row, work 1 half-dc in following st. Repeat from * across the row.

Following rows: Repeat Row 2.

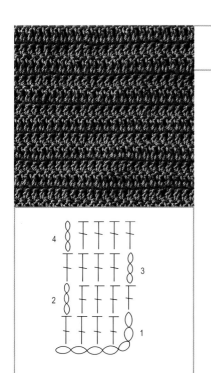

DOUBLE CROCHET

Work a base chain with as many chain stitches as you need for the width.

Row 1: 3 ch (to count as first dc of row), skip 1 ch st, * work 1 dc in following stitch. Repeat from * across the row.

Row 2: 3 ch (= 1 dc), skip 1 st, * work 1 dc in following st. Repeat from * across the row.

Following rows: Repeat Row 2.

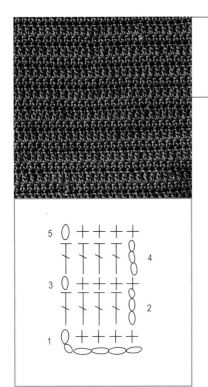

SINGLE CROCHET PLUS DOUBLE CROCHET

Work a base chain with as many chain stitches as you need for the width.

Row 1 (ws): 1 ch, skip 2 ch sts, * work 1 sc in following stitch. Repeat from * across the row.

Row 2 (rs): 3 ch (= to count as 1st dc), skip 1 st, * work 1 dc in following st. Repeat from * across the row. End by working 1 dc in 1st ch st at beg of preceding row.

Row 3: 1 ch, skip 1 st, * work 1 sc in following st. Repeat from * across the row. End by working 1 sc in 3rd ch st at beg of preceding row.

Following rows: Repeat Rows 2 and 3.

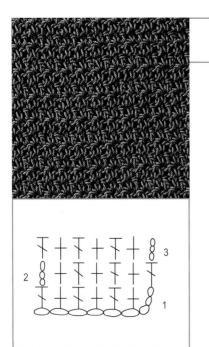

TOLEWARE STITCH

Work chain stitches for a base chain in a multiple of 2 stitches plus 1 stitch.

Row 1: 2 ch, skip 3 ch sts, * work 1 sc in next st, 1 dc in following stitch. Repeat from * across the row. End by working 1 sc in last ch st.

Row 2: 3 ch, skip 1 st, now * work 1 sc in next sc, 1 dc over foll dc*. Repeat from * to * across the row. End by working 1 dc in 3rd ch st at beg of preceding row.

Following rows: Repeat Row 2.

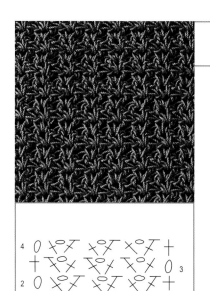

RIDDLE STITCH

Work chain stitches for a base chain in a multiple of 3 stitches plus 2 stitches.

Row 1: 1 ch, skip 2 ch sts, * work (1 sc, 1 ch, 1 dc) in next ch st, skip 2 ch sts *. Repeat from * to * across the row. End by working 1 sc in last ch st of row.

Row 2: 1 ch, * work (1 sc, 1 ch, 1 dc) in 1-st chain lp *. Repeat from * to * across the row. End by working 1 sc in ch st at beg of preceding row.

Following rows: Repeat Row 2.

GRANITE STITCH

Work chain stitches for a base chain in a multiple of 2.

Row 1: 3 ch, skip 3 ch sts, work 1 sc in next ch st, * 1 dc in foll ch st, 1 sc in next ch st *. Repeat from * to * across the row. End by working 1 sc in last ch st of row.

Row 2: 3 ch, skip 1 st, * work 1 sc over next dc, 1 dc over foll sc *. Repeat from * to * across the row. End by working 1 sc in 3rd ch st at beg of preceding row.

Following rows: Repeat Row 2.

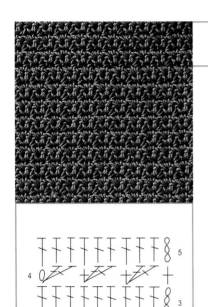

SAND STITCH

Work chain stitches for a base chain in a multiple of 3.

Row 1 (rs): 3 ch, skip 3 ch sts, work 1 dc in each following ch st.

Row 2 (ws): 1 ch, work 2 dc over first st of row, skip 2 sts, * work (1 sc, 2 dc) in foll st, skip 2 sts *. Repeat from * to * across the row. End by working 1 sc over 3rd ch st at beg of preceding row.

Row 3: 3 ch, skip 1 st, now work 1 dc over each st in the preceding row. End with 1 dc in ch st at beg of preceding row.

Following rows: Repeat Rows 2 and 3.

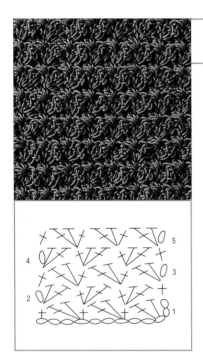

STARRY STITCH

Work a base chain with a multiple of 3 stitches plus 1 stitch.

Row 1: 2 ch, skip 2 ch sts, work (1 half-dc, 1 dc) in next ch st, skip 2 ch sts, then * work (1 sc, 1 half-dc, 1 dc) in next ch st, skip 2 sts *, rep from * to * across the row. End with 1 sc over the last ch st.

Row 2: 1 ch, work (1 half-dc, 1 dc) in 1st st of row, then * skip 2 sts, work (1 sc, 1 half-dc, 1 dc) in next st *, rep from * to * across the row. End by working 1 sc over 2nd ch st at beg of preceding row.

Following rows: Repeat Row 2.

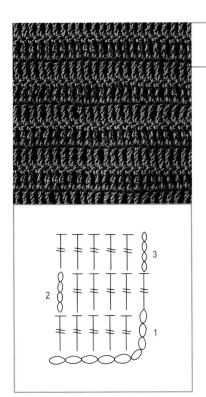

TREBLE CROCHET STITCH

Work a base chain with as many chain stitches as you need for the width.

Row 1: 4 ch, skip 4 ch sts, work 1 tr in foll st, and work 1 tr in each st across the row.

Row 2: 4 ch, skip the next tr in the preceding row, and * into foll st work 1 tr. Rep from * across the row.

Following rows: Rep Row 2.

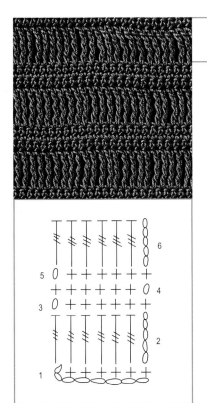

TRAIL STITCH

Work a base chain with as many chain stitches as you need for the width.

Row 1 (ws): 1 ch, skip 1 ch st, work 1 sc in each foll st of the base chain.

Row 2 (rs): 5 ch, skip 1 st, work 1 dbl tr into each sc of the preceding row. End by working 1 dbl tr over the ch st at beg of preceding row.

Rows 3–5: 1 ch, skip 1 st, work 1 sc in each st of the preceding row. End by working 1 sc over the ch st at beg of previous row.

Following rows: Rep Rows 2–5.

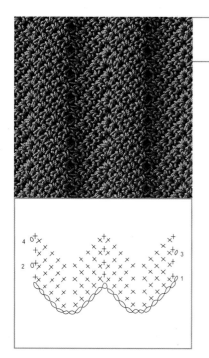

CHEVRONS IN SINGLE CROCHET

Work a base chain with a multiple of 11 chain stitches plus 1 stitch.

Row 1 (rs): 1 ch, 2 sc over 2nd ch st from hook, * work 1 sc in each of the next 4 ch sts, skip 2 ch sts, 1 sc in each of the foll 4 ch sts, 3 sc in foll ch st *, rep from * to * across the row. End the row by working 2 sc over the last ch st.

Row 2 (ws): 1 ch, 2 sc in 1st st of row, then work * 1 sc in each of the next 4 sts, skip 2 sc, 1 sc in each of the next 4 sts, 3 sc in foll st *, rep from * to * across the row. End the row by working 2 sc over the last ch st.

Following rows: Rep Row 2.

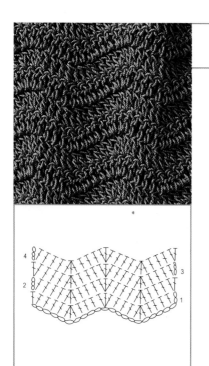

CHEVRONS IN DOUBLE CROCHET

Work a base chain with a multiple of 10 chain stitches plus 1 stitch.

Row 1: 3 ch (to count as first dc), 1 dc over next ch st, * work 1 dc in each of the next 3 ch sts, 3 dc tog over foll 3 ch sts, 1 dc in each of the next 3 ch sts, 3 dc in foll ch st *, rep from * to * across the row. End the row by working 2 dc tog over the last ch st.

Row 2: 3 ch (to count as first dc), 1 dc in 1st st of row, then work * 1 dc in each of the next 3 sts, 3 dc tog, 1 dc in each of the next 3 sts, 3 dc in foll st *, rep from * to * across the row. End the row by working 2 dc over the last dc.

Following rows: Rep Row 2.

RIBBED CHEVRONS

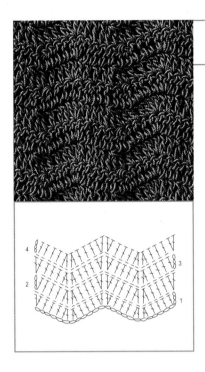

Work a base chain with a multiple of 12 chain stitches.

Row 1: 3 ch (to count as first dc), 1 dc over next ch st, * work 1 dc in each of the next 3 ch sts, ° * work (2 dc tog over foll 2 ch sts) *, rep from * to *, 1 dc in each of the next 3 ch sts, ** work (2 dc in foll ch st) ** rep from ** to ** °, rep from ° to ° across the row. End the row by working 2 dc over the last ch st.

Row 2: 3 ch (to count as first dc), 1 dc in 1st st, then, working through back strand only of each st in the preceding row, cont with * 1 dc in each of the next 3 sts, * (2 dc tog over next 2 sts) *, rep from * to *, 1 dc in each of the next 3 sts, ** (2 dc in foll st) **, rep from ° to ° across the row. End the row by working 2 dc over the last st.

Following rows: Rep Row 2.

Bucket bag

BUCKET BAG

Materials

4 50g balls of Gedifra "Korella" (53% linen, 47% acrylic)

Olive no. 8407.

1 3 mm crochet hook

Lining: toning printed fabric measuring 12 X 36 in [30 X 90 cm].

Green sewing thread

1 darning needle

1 crewel needle

pins

1 safety pin

Size

Finished bag measures 8-¼ in tall X 8-¼ in diameter [21 X 21 cm] not counting the handle

Stitches used

Single crochet (p. 47)

Trail stitch (p. 53)

Skill level

** Some experience

TO MAKE

BAG

Work 106 ch sts for a base chain.

Work 3 rows of single crochet, then continue in trail stitch until bag measures 8 in [20 cm] from base chain = 5 rows of double trebles. Work in single crochet for another 3 rows, then fasten off.

BASE

Work 4 ch for a base chain. Work 1 sl st into the first of the 4 ch sts to form a ring. Work Rnd 1 into the ring thus formed.

Rnd 1: 1 ch, then into ring work 8 sc. Close by working 1 sl st over the ch st at beg of rnd.

Rnd 2: 1 ch (to count as first sc of rnd), 1 sc in foll st, then work 2 sc in each of the next 7 sts = 16 sts. Close by working 1 sl st over the ch st at beg of rnd.

Rnd 3: 1 ch (to count as first sc of rnd). Place a safety pin to mark the st at the beg of the rnd; move the safety pin up a row or two from time to time as the base grows. Work 1 sc over next st, then work * 2 sc in next st and 1 sc in foll st *. Rep from * to * to end of rnd = 24 sts. End by working 1 sl st over the ch st at beg of rnd.

Rnd 4: 1 ch (= 1 sc), 1 sc in next st, then * 2 sc in next st, and 1 sc in each of foll 2 sts *, rep from * to * = 32 sts. End by working 1 sl st over ch st at beg of rnd.

Rnd 5: 1 ch (= 1 sc), 1 sc in next st, then * 2 sc in next st, and 1 sc in each of foll 3 sts *, rep from * to * = 40 sts. End by working 1 sl st over ch st at beg of rnd.

Rnd 6: 1 ch (= 1 sc), 1 sc in next st, then * 2 sc in next st, and 1 sc in each of foll 4 sts *, rep from * to * = 48 sts. End by working 1 sl st over ch st at beg of rnd.

Rnd 7: 1 ch (= 1 sc), 1 sc in next st, then * 2 sc in next st, and 1 sc in each of foll 5 sts *, rep from * to * = 56 sts. End by working 1 sl st over ch st at beg of rnd.

Rnds 8–21: Continue as established, progressively working an extra single crochet with each increase of (2 sc in foll st), until you have 168 sts. Fasten off.

HANDLE

Work 60 ch sts for a base chain.

Rows 1–10: 1 ch (= 1 sc), then work 1 sc over each st of preceding row. At completion of Row 10, fasten off.

MAKING THE BAG

1. Darn in all the yarn ends.

2. Following the chart, fold the bag in half, rs tog, and join by overcasting (p. 37), using the darning needle and the crochet yarn. Turn the cylinder thus formed right side out and fit the base into the bag; pin it in position. With rs of bag facing, work 1 row of sc through both thicknesses to join bag and base.

3. From the lining fabric cut a rectangle measuring 9 X 19 in [23 X 48 cm], a circle 9 in [23 cm] in diameter, and a strip measuring 2-1/2 X 14 in [6 X 36 cm].

4. Press 1/2 in [1 cm] to the wrong side on each side of the strip. Pin the strip to the handle and slipstitch the long edges using the green sewing thread.

5. Using the green thread, backstitch the ends of the handles on opposite sides of the bag, at the inside top edge.

6. Fold the lining rectangle in half, rs tog, and stitch a 1/2 in [1 cm] seam. Pin the fabric circle into one end of the lining cylinder and stitch 1/2 in [1 cm] from the edge. Trim the seam allowance with pinking shears to prevent fraying, and press the seams open.

7. Place the lining in the bag, ws tog. Fold 1/2 in [1 cm] to the ws at the top edge of the lining. Slipstitch the lining in place using the green thread.

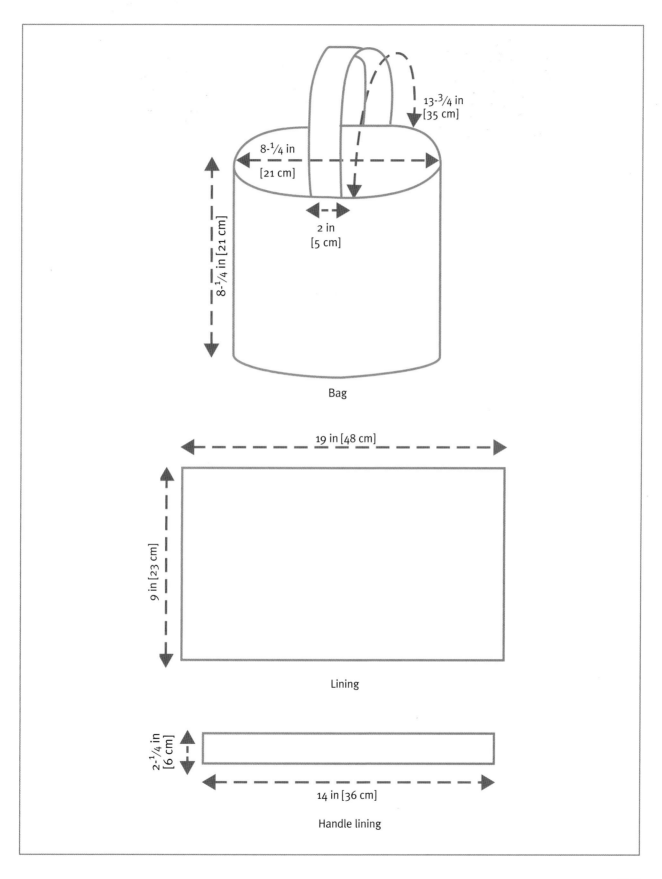

8-1/4 in [21 cm]

13-3/4 in [35 cm]

8-1/4 in [21 cm]

2 in [5 cm]

Bag

19 in [48 cm]

9 in [23 cm]

Lining

2-1/4 in [6 cm]

14 in [36 cm]

Handle lining

Carry-all

CARRY-ALL

Materials

4 50g balls of Gedifra "Korella" (53% linen, 47% acrylic)

Kaki no. 8467.

1 3 mm crochet hook

Lining: toning printed fabric measuring 12 X 36 in [30 X 90 cm].

Khaki sewing thread

1 darning needle

1 crewel needle

pins

Size

Finished carry-all measures 8-¼ in tall X 1-¼ in deep X 10 in wide [21 X 4 X 25 cm] not counting the handle

Stitches used

Single crochet (p. 47)

Starry stitch (p. 52)

Skill level

* Beginner

TO MAKE

BACK AND FRONT

Work 46 ch sts for a base chain.

Rows 1–8: 1 ch (to count as first sc of row), then 1 sc over each st of previous row.

Rows 9–16: Follow the instructions for starry stitch on p. 52.

Rows 17–24: 1 ch (to count as first sc of row), then 1 sc over each st of previous row.

Rows 25–32: Follow the instructions for starry stitch on p. 52.

Rows 33–40: 1 ch (to count as first sc of row), then 1 sc over each st of previous row. At the completion of Row 40, fasten off.

Make a second, identical piece for the other side of the bag.

BASE

Work 46 ch sts for a base chain.

Rows 1–10: 1 ch (to count as first sc of row), then 1 sc over each st of previous row. At the completion of Row 10, fasten off.

GUSSETS (MAKE 2)

Work 37 ch sts for a base chain.

Rows 1–8: 1 ch (to count as first sc of row), then 1 sc over each st of previous row. At the completion of Row 8, fasten off.

Complete a second, identical gusset.

HANDLES (MAKE 2)

Work 65 ch sts for a base chain.

Rows 1–8: 1 ch (to count as first sc of row), then 1 sc over each st of previous row. At the completion of Row 8, fasten off.

Complete a second, identical handle.

MAKING THE CARRY-ALL

1. Darn in all the yarn ends.

2. Pin the base to the back and front, ws tog, matching stitch for stitch and, with rs facing, work 1 row of single crochets to join the 3 sections.

Pin the gussets at each end of the carry-all and join with single crochets as for the other sections.

3. From the lining fabric cut 2 rectangles measuring 9 X 10-½ in [23 X 27 cm], another rectangle 2-¼ X 10-½ in [6 X 27 cm] for the base, 2 strips measuring 2-½ X 9 in [6 X 23 cm] for the gussets, and another 2 strips measuring 2-½ X 14 in [6 X 36 cm] for the handles.

4. Press ½ in [1 cm] to the wrong side on each edge of the handle strips. Pin the strips to the handles, ws tog, and slipstitch the long edges using the khaki sewing thread.

5. Using the khaki thread, backstitch the ends of the handles on the back and front of the carry-all, 1-¼ in [3 cm] from each end, as shown in the chart.

6. Pin the lining rectangles to the strip for the base and stitch ½ in [1 cm] from the edge. Fit the gussets into the lining and stitch as before. Press the seams open and trim the corners with pinking shears to prevent fraying. Place the lining in the carry-all, ws tog. Fold ½ in [1 cm] to the ws at the top edge of the lining. Slipstitch the lining in place using the khaki thread.

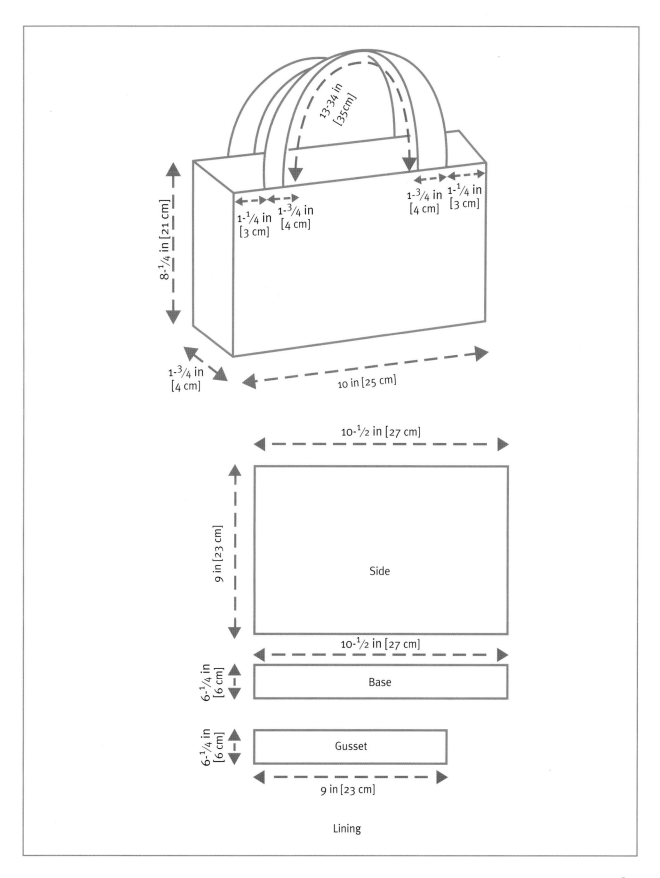

13-34 in [35cm]

1-1/4 in [3 cm]

1-3/4 in [4 cm]

1-3/4 in [4 cm]

1-1/4 in [3 cm]

8-1/4 in [21 cm]

1-3/4 in [4 cm]

10 in [25 cm]

10-1/2 in [27 cm]

9 in [23 cm]

Side

10-1/2 in [27 cm]

6-1/4 in [6 cm]

Base

6-1/4 in [6 cm]

Gusset

9 in [23 cm]

Lining

Baby pullover

BABY PULLOVER

Materials

3 balls of Rowan "Soft 4-ply" yarn (100% merino wool)

Linseed no. 393.

1 3 mm crochet hook

3 small shell buttons

1 darning needle

Pins

Size

Newborn—3 months –6 months

Instructions for larger sizes are shown in parentheses. When only one number is given, it applies to all sizes.

Stitches used

Double crochet (p. 49)

Single crochet (p.47)

Granite stitch (p. 51)

Skill level

** Some experience

TO MAKE

FRONT

Work 49 (53, 61) sts for a base chain. Follow the instructions on p. 51 to work in granite st for 3 rows.

Row 4: Eyelet pattern: 4 ch, skip 1 st, * 1 dc in next st, 1 ch, skip 1 st *, rep from * to * across the row. End by working 1 dc after the last dc of the eyelets.

Cont straight in granite stitch until front measures approximately 9-$\frac{1}{2}$ (10-$\frac{1}{2}$–12$\frac{1}{4}$) in [24.5 (27–31) cm] from base chain.

Neck: Next row: Pattern across 14 (16-20) sts; turn the work. Complete the 2 sides separately from this point, beg with left front. Work straight in rows of granite stitch until left front measures approximately $\frac{1}{2}$ in [1.5 cm] from the dividing row. The front now measures approximately 10-$\frac{1}{4}$ (11-$\frac{1}{4}$—12-$\frac{3}{4}$) in [26 (28.5—32.5) cm] from the base chain. Fasten off.

Leaving the 21 central sts unworked, rejoin the yarn with a sl st in the foll st and complete the right front to match.

BACK (MAKE 2)

Work 24 (26-30) ch sts for a base chain and work in granite st for 3 rows.

Row 4: Eyelet pattern: 4 ch, skip 1 st, * 1 dc in next st, 1 ch, skip 1 st *, rep from * to * across the row. End by working 1 dc after the last dc of the eyelets.

Cont straight in granite stitch until back measures approximately 9-$\frac{3}{4}$ (10-$\frac{3}{4}$–12-$\frac{1}{4}$) in [24.5 (27–31) cm from base chain. Fasten off. Complete a second, identical back.

SLEEVES (MAKE 2)

Work 35 (39, 45) ch sts for a base chain. Work in granite st for 3 rows.

Row 4: Eyelet pattern: 4 ch, skip-1 st, * 1 dc in next st, 1 ch, skip 1 st *, rep from * to * across the row. End by working 1 dc after the last dc of the eyelets.

Cont straight in granite st to the end of Row 10 (11–13).

Next row: Follow the instructions on p. 26 to increase 1 st at end of the row.

Continuing in granite stitch, repeat these increases every 3 rows 4 (6–8) more times until you have 45 (53–63) sts.

Work straight for another 5 (7–10) rows.

Next row: Eyelet pattern: 4 ch, skip 1 st, * 1 dc in next st, 1 ch, skip 1 st *, rep from * to * across the row. End by working 1 dc after the last dc of the eyelets.

Next row: Work in sc across row. Fasten off.

Complete a second, identical sleeve.

MAKING THE PULLOVER

Darn in all the yarn ends.

Pin front to backs, rs tog, and backstitch the shoulders, then backstitch the side seams 4 (4-3/4 –5-1/2) in [10 (12–14 cm]), working up from the base chain.

Fold each sleeve in half lengthways. Fit the top of each sleeve into the opening left at the top of each side seam. Backstitch in place, then backstitch the sleeve seams.

On left back, using the needle and yarn, work 3 buttonhole loops: attach yarn with a sl st then work a few sts 3 dc ahead, forming a 2-strand loop; work back over this loop by embroidering buttonhole stitch (see detail chart). Work the first button loop at the neck edge and the others 2 in [5 cm] apart. Sew the shell button on right back opposite the button loops.

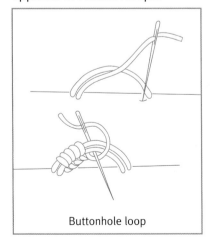

Buttonhole loop

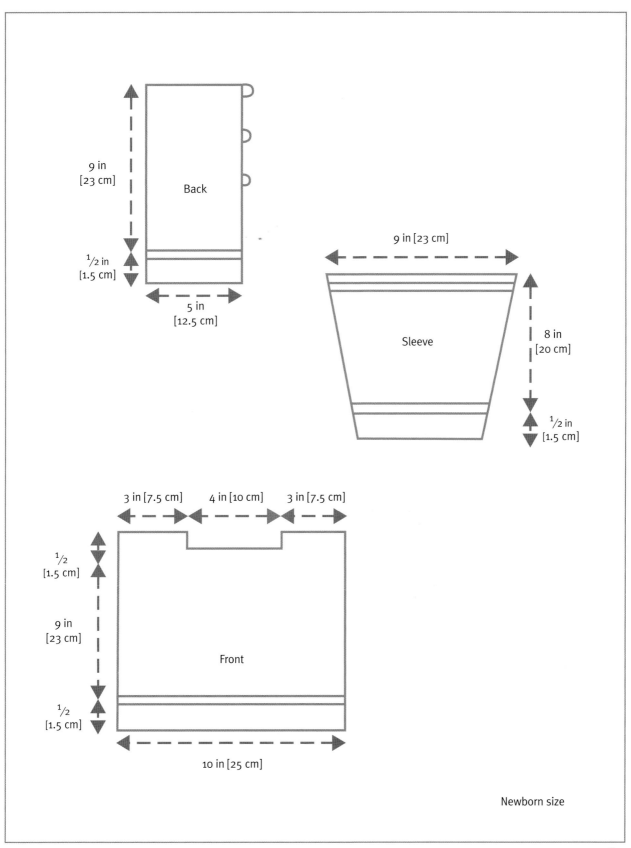

9 in
[23 cm]

Back

¹/₂ in
[1.5 cm]

5 in
[12.5 cm]

9 in [23 cm]

Sleeve

8 in
[20 cm]

¹/₂ in
[1.5 cm]

3 in [7.5 cm]   4 in [10 cm]   3 in [7.5 cm]

¹/₂
[1.5 cm]

9 in
[23 cm]

Front

¹/₂
[1.5 cm]

10 in [25 cm]

Newborn size

Cuddly toy

CUDDLY TOY

Materials

2 balls of Coats "Aida" no. 10 cotton yarn (100% cotton)

Ficelle no. 390 and Myosotis no. 117.

1 2 mm crochet hook

1 darning needle

Synthetic batting

Pins

Size

The body of the finished toy measures approximately:

3 in wide X 12 in long (8 X 30 cm).

Stitches used

Single crochet (p. 47)

Skill level

*** Experienced

TO MAKE

FRONT OF THE HEAD (beg with the nose)

Using Myosotis, work 4 ch, close with a sl st to form a ring.

Rnd 1: 1 ch, then into ring work 7 sc, close with 1 sl st in ch st at beg of rnd.

Rnds 2–4: 1 ch, *1 sc in next st, 2 sc in foll st *, rep from * to * to end of rnd, close with sl st in ch st at beg of rnd.

Rnds 5–11: 1 ch, work 1 dc over each sc of preceding rnd, close with 1 sl st over ch st at beg of rnd.

Rnd 12: 1 ch, * 1 sc over each of the next 5 sts, then into foll st work (1 sc, 1 ch, 1 sc) *, rep from * to * to end; close with a sl st over 1st ch st of rnd. Tie a contrasting yarn marker to indicate the ch st (inc st).

Rnds 13–16: 1 ch, 1 sc over each sc of preceding rnd, then over inc ch st of previous rnd work (1 sc, 1 ch, 1 sc). Close each rnd with 1 sl st over the first ch st of rnd. At completion of Rnd 16, fasten off. Remove the contrasting yarn markers.

BACK OF THE HEAD

Using Ficelle, work 4 ch sts and close with a sl st to form a ring.

Rnd 1: 1 ch, 7 sc into ring, 1 sl st in first of the ch sts at beg of rnd.

Rnds 2–4: 1 ch, * 1 sc in next st, 1 sc in foll st *, rep from * to * to end, close with 1 sl st over ch st at beg of rnd.

Rnd 5: 1 ch, * 1 sc over each of the next 2 sts, 2 sc in foll st *, rep from * to *. Close with 1 sl st over ch st at beg of rnd.

Rnd 6: 1 ch, * 1 sc in each of next 4 sts 2 sc in foll st *, rep from * to *. Close with a sl st over ch st at beg of rnd.

Rnds 7–9: 1 ch, 1 sc over each sc of previous rnd, close with a sl st over ch st at beg of rnd.

Rnd 10: 1 ch, * 1 sc in each of next 10 sts, 2 sc in foll st *, rep from * to *. Close with a sl st over ch st at beg of rnd.

Rnd 11: 1 ch, 1 sc over each st of previous rnd. Close with a sl st over ch st at beg of rnd.

Rnd 12: 1 ch, * 1 sc in each of next 10 sts, 2 sc in foll st *, rep from * to *. Close with a sl st over ch st at beg of rnd.

Rnd 13: 1 ch, 1 sc over each st of previous rnd. Close with a sl st over ch st at beg of rnd. Fasten off.

EARS (MAKE 2):

Using Ficelle, work 4 ch and join with a sl st to form a ring.

Rnd 1: 1 ch, then work 6 sc over half of ring; turn the work with ws facing Continue working over the half-circle thus formed.

Rows 2–4: 1 ch, * 1 sc in next st, 2 sc in foll st *, rep from * to * to end; turn the work.

Rows 5–7: 1 ch, then 1 sc over each st. At completion of Row 7, fasten off.

Complete a second, identical ear.

BODY

Using Ficelle, work 29 ch sts for a base chain.

Rows 1–30: 1 ch, then 1 sc over each st of previous row. Now shape the neck as follows.

Neck:

Row 31: 1 ch, 1 sc in each of next 13 sts, then dec as follows: skip 1 st, work 1 sc in foll st, skip 1 st. Close the row by working 1 sc over each of last 13 sts.

Row 32: 1 ch, 1 sc over each of next 12 sts, then dec as follows: skip 1 st, work 1 sc in foll st, skip 1 st. Close by working 1 sc in each of last 12 sts.

Row 33: 1 ch, 11 sc, then dec as follows: skip 1 st, work 1 sc in foll st, skip 1 st. Close with 1 sc in each of last 11 sts.

Row 34: 1 ch, 1 sc in each of next 10 sc. Now dec as follows: skip 1 st, work 1 sc in foll st, skip 1 st. Close with 1 sc in each of last 10 sc.

Row 35: 1 ch, 1 sc in each of next 9 sc. Now dec as follows: skip 1 st, work 1 sc in foll st, skip 1 st. Close with 1 sc in each of last 9 sc.

Row 36: 1 ch, 1 sc in each of next 8 sc. Now dec as follows: skip 1 st, work 1 sc in foll st, skip 1 st. Close with 1 sc in each of last 8 sc.

Row 37: 1 ch, 1 sc over each st of previous row. On completing Row 37, fasten off.

Complete a second, identical rectangle.

LEGS (MAKE 2)

Using Ficelle, work 20 ch sts for a base chain.

Alternating 4 rows Ficelle and 4 rows Myosotis, work every row as follows: 1 ch, 1 sc over each st of previous row. Beg and end each leg with 4 rows Ficelle. Each leg will thus have 12 rows Myosotis.

Complete a second, identical leg.

ARMS (MAKE 2)

Work as given for the legs, with 10 (instead of 12) stripes in Myosotis.

POUCH

Using Ficelle, work 15 ch sts for a base chain and work each row as follows: 1 ch, 1 sc over each st of preceding row.

Work 2 rows Ficelle and 2 rows Myosotis alternately. The pouch will thus have 4 stripes in Myosotis.

Pouch border: Rejoin Myosotis with a sl st on one side of the pouch, and work 3 rows in single crochet for a border. Fasten off.

Darn in all the yarn ends then join up the various sections.

ASSEMBLY

Use Ficelle yarn to join the sections of the toy.

HEAD
Pin back and front rs tog. Backstitch the curved seam, leaving an opening about 1-3/4 in [4 cm] long at the neck.
Turn the head rs out and stuff the head with synthetic batting. Close up the seam with a few tacking stitches.
Position the ears on either side of the head with pins pointing straight downward. Slipstitch the ears in place.

LEGS AND ARMS
Fold each strip lengthways, ws tog, and work 1 row of sc through both thicknesses to form the 4 limbs.

BODY
Center the pouch on 1 rectangle, 3/4 in [1.5 cm] from the lower edge, with the blue border at the top. Slipstitch 3 sides, leaving the pouch open at the top.
Place the 2 body sections ws together. Pin on 3 sides, leaving the neck open. Slip the end of each limb (arms and legs) between back and front, making sure that you place the finishing row of single crochets toward the back of the toy. With rs facing, close up the seams by backstitching with a needle and thread. Make sure that you work through all thicknesses when attaching the arms and legs.
Stuff the body with batting. With rs facing, push the head a little (a few millimeters) down into the neck and attach it firmly by backstitching with a needle and thread.

FINISHING

Tie the end of each limb into a knot (see photo). Using a double strand of Myosotis, embroider a cross stitch to form each eye.

Baby booties

MARY-JANE BOOTIES

Materials

1 50g ball of Rowan "Cotton Wool" yarn (50% merino wool, 50% cotton)

Grand no. 954.

1 3 mm crochet hook

2 little buttons

Sizes

3 months –6 months

Stitches used

Single crochet (p.47)

Crab stitch (p. 45)

Starry stitch (p. 52)

Skill level

* Beginner

TO MAKE

MARY-JANE BOOTIES

Work 3 ch sts, join with a sl st to form a ring.

Work the sole of the bootie in rounds as follows:

Rnd 1: 1 ch, into ring work 8 sc. Close with a sl st over first ch st of rnd.

Rnd 2: 1 ch, 2 sc in each st = 16 sc. Close with a sl st over first ch st of rnd.

Rnd 3: 1 ch, * 1 sc in next st, 2 sc in foll st*, rep from * to * = 24 sc. Close with a sl st over first ch st of rnd.

3 months:

Rnds 4–9: 1 ch, then 1 sc over each sc. Close with a sl st over ch st at beg of rnd.

Row 10: Work forward with a sl st in each of next 4 sts, then work back and forth in rows of starry stitch over the central 16 sts to the end of Row 16. Fasten off.

6 months:

Rnd 4: 1 ch, * 1 sc in each of next 5 sts, 2 sc in foll st *, rep from * to * = 28 sc

Close with a sl st over ch st at beg of rnd.

Rnds 5–12: 1 ch, then 1 sc over each sc. Close with a sl st over ch st at beg of rnd.

Work forward with a sl st in each of next 4 sts, then work back and forth in 9 rows of starry stitch over the central 20 sts to the end of Row 21. Fasten off.

MARY-JANE BOOTIES

HEEL

3 months:
Work 4 ch for a base chain.
Rows 1–4: 1 ch, 1 sc over each sc = 4 sc.
Row 5: 1 ch, 1 sc over each of next 3 sc, turn the work (= 1 dec).
Row 6: 1 ch, 1 sc over each of next 3 sts, 1 sl st in last st. Fasten off.

6 months:
Work 5 ch for a base chain.
Rows 1–5: 1 ch, 1 sc over each sc = 5 sc.
Row 6: 1 ch, 1 sc over each of next 4 sc, turn the work (= 1 dec).
Row 7: 1 ch, 1 sc over each of next 4 sts, 1 sl st in last st. Fasten off.

Both sizes:
Curve the sole of the bootie into a U shape and fit the heel to it with the flat section of the heel at the top. Work 1 row of crab stitch (sc from left to right) to join the seam.

STRAP
Both sizes:
Rejoin the yarn with a sl st 2 sts along the upper of the bootie on the inner side. Work 12 ch sts. * Work back over the ch sts with 1 sc in each st. Rep from * = 2 rows of sc. Close Row 2 with a sl st at the edge of the bootie, next to the sl st where you joined the yarn. Fasten off.
Work an identical strap beginning on the inside of the other bootie.
Sew a little button on the other side of each bootie and draw it between the sts to fasten the bootie.

HIGH-TOP BOOTIES

Materials

1 50g ball of Rowan "Cotton Wool" yarn (50% merino wool, 50% cotton)

Riviera no. 930, plus a remnant (about 2 yards) of Grand no. 954.

1 3 mm crochet hook

1 darning or tapestry needle

Sizes

3 months –6 months

Instructions for the larger size are shown in parentheses. Where only one number appears, it applies to both sizes.

Stitches used

Single crochet (p.47)

Crab stitch (p. 45)

Starry stitch (p. 52)

Skill level

** Some experience

TO MAKE

HIGH-TOP BOOTIES

SOLE (MAKE 2)

3 months:

Using Riviera, work 10 ch sts, then work around this base chain to form an oval as follows:

Rnd 1: 3 ch, 10 sc (1 in each st of base chain), 3 ch, then 10 sc along the other side of the base chain. Close with a sl st over the ch st at beg of rnd.

Rnd 2: 1 ch, into chain loop work (1 sc, 1 ch, 1 sc), then 1 sc over each of the next 11 sc. In foll chain lp work (1 sc, 1 ch, 1 sc), then 1 sc in each of the foll 11 sc. Close with a sl st over the ch st at beg of rnd.

Rnd 3: 1 ch, into chain lp work (1 sc, 1 ch, 1 sc), then cont with 1 sc over each of the next 12 sc. In foll chain lp work (1 sc, 1 ch, 1 sc), then 1 sc in each of the foll 12 sc. Close with a sl st over the ch st at beg of rnd. Fasten off.

Make another, identical sole.

6 months:

Using Riviera, work 12 ch sts, then work around this base chain to form an oval as follows:

Rnd 1: 3 ch, 12 sc (1 in each st of base chain), 3 ch, then 12 sc along the other side of the base chain. Close with a sl st over the ch st at beg of rnd.

Rnd 2: 1 ch, into chain loop work (1 sc, 1 ch, 1 sc), then 1 sc over each of the next 13 sc. In foll chain lp work (1 sc, 1 ch, 1 sc), then 1 sc in each of the foll 13 sc. Close with a sl st over the ch st at beg of rnd.

Rnd 3: 1 ch, into chain lp work (1 sc, 1 ch, 1 sc), then cont with 1 sc over each of the next 14 sc. In foll chain lp work (1 sc, 1 ch, 1 sc), then 1 sc in each of the foll 14 sc. Close with a sl st over the ch st at beg of rnd. Fasten off.

Make another, identical sole.

HIGH-TOP BOOTIES

BOOTIE SIDES (MAKE 2)

Both sizes: Using Riviera, work 39 (43) ch sts for a base chain and continue with 4 (5) rows of starry stitch (work 1 st over each st of previous row). Fasten off. Make another, identical side.
Place the side against the sole, ws tog (see chart) and, beg at center heel with rs facing, work 1 rnd of crab stitch (sc from left to right, st over st). Turn the bootie inside out to backstitch the back seam.

BOOTIE UPPER (MAKE 2)

Both sizes:
Rows 1–4: Using Riviera, work 6 (8) ch sts for a base chain and continue with 4 (5) rows of single crochet (work 1 st over each st of previous row

3 months:
Row 5: 1 ch, 1 sc over each of next 5 sts, turn the work.
Row 6: 1 ch, 1 sc over each of next 4 sts. Fasten off.

6 months:
Row 6: 1 ch, 1 sc over each of next 7 sts, turn the work.
Row 7: 1 ch, 1 sc over each of next 6 sts, turn the work.
Row 8: 1 ch, 1 sc over each of next 5 sts, turn the work. Fasten off.

Both sizes:
Place the upper in the toe of the bootie, ws tog (see chart) and, with rs facing backstitch the seam using a strand of Grand.

HIGH-TOP (MAKE 2)

Both sizes:
Rejoin the Riviera yarn with a sl at the top of the heel seam. Work 1 sl st in each of the 32 (36) sts around the sides and across the upper. Turn the work. Now continuing in starry stitch, work 4 (5) rows in Riviera, 1 row in Grand, 1 row in Riviera. Fasten off.
Backstitch the seam.

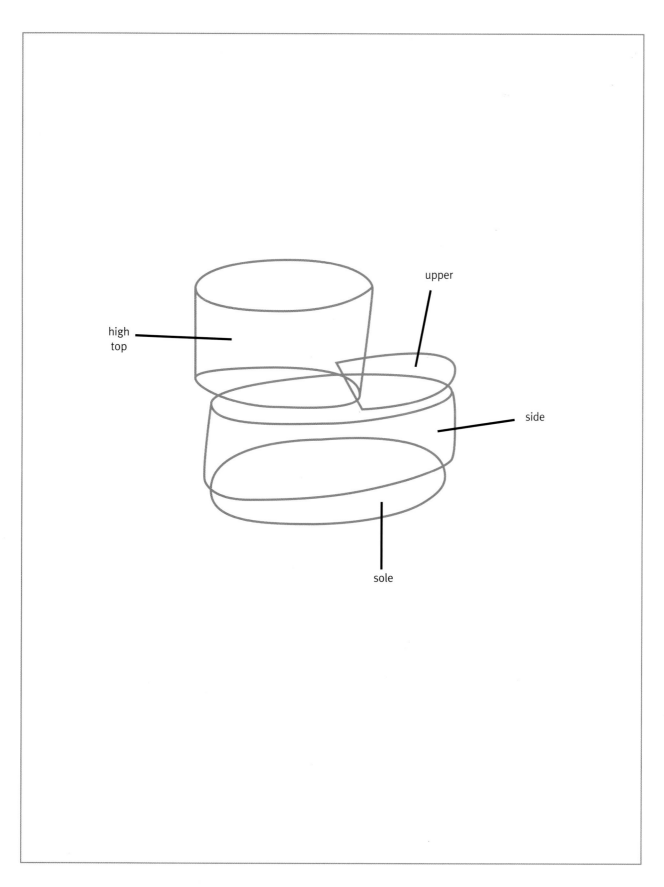

top

upper

side

sole

Jacket in ribbed single crochet

JACKET IN RIBBED SINGLE CROCHET

Materials

11 (12) 25g balls of Rowan "Scottish Tweed" 4-ply yarn (100% wool)

Grey Mist no. 01.

1 4 mm crochet hook

1 darning or tapestry needle

9 shell buttons ½ in [1.5 cm] in diameter

Sizes

US 8/10 (EUR 38/40) —12/14 (42/44)

Instructions for the larger size are shown in parentheses. Where only one number appears, it applies to both sizes.

Stitches used

Ribbed single crochet (p.47)

To obtain the horizontal ribbing effect, work half-dc through back strand only of each st in preceding row.

Single crochet (p. 47)

Skill level

*** Experienced

TO MAKE

BACK

Work 83 (89) ch sts for a base chain, then work 4 rows as follows: 1 ch, then 1 sc over each st of preceding row.

Row 5: Continue in ribbed sc (working through back strand only of each st in preceding row), st over st. Work straight in ribbed sc until back measures 13-³/₄ (14-¹/₂) in [35 (37)cm] from base chain. **Armholes: Next row:** Work 1 sl st in each of next 3 sts, cont in ribbed sc until 3 sts remain, turn the work. **Next row:** * Work 1 sl st in each of next 2 sts, cont in ribbed sc until 2 sts remain, turn the work *. Rep from * to *. **Next row:** ** Work 1 sl st in next st, cont in ribbed sc until 1 st remains, turn the work **. Rep from ** to ** = 65 (71) sts. Cont straight in ribbed sc until back measures 21-¹/₄ (21-³/₄) in [54 (55) cm] from base chain. **Neck and shoulders: Next row:** Work 23 (26) sts, turn. Complete the 2 sides separately from this point, beg with right back. Work back to armhole edge. **Next row:** Work 1 sl st in each of next 9 (10) sts, cont to end of row = 14 (16) sts remain. Work 1 row straight. **Next row:** Work 1 sl st in each of next 8 (9) sts, cont to end of row = 6 (7) sts remain. Work 1 row straight. **Next row:** Work 1 sl st in each of remaining sts. Fasten off. **Left back:** Count 19 sts across center back, beg where you divided for right and left back. Rejoin the yarn with a sl st in foll st and complete the left back as given for the right, reversing the shaping.

RIGHT FRONT:

Work 42 (45) ch sts for a base chain, then work 4 rows as follows: 1 ch, then 1 sc over each st of preceding row.

Row 5: Continue in ribbed sc (working through back strand only of each st in preceding row), st over st. Work straight in ribbed sc until right front measures 13-³/₄ (14-¹/₂) in [35 (37) cm] from base chain. **Armhole: Next row:** With ws facing, work 1 sl st in each of next 3 sts, cont in ribbed sc to end of row, turn the work. **Next row:** * Work 1 sl st in each of next 2 sts, cont in ribbed sc to end of row, turn the work *.

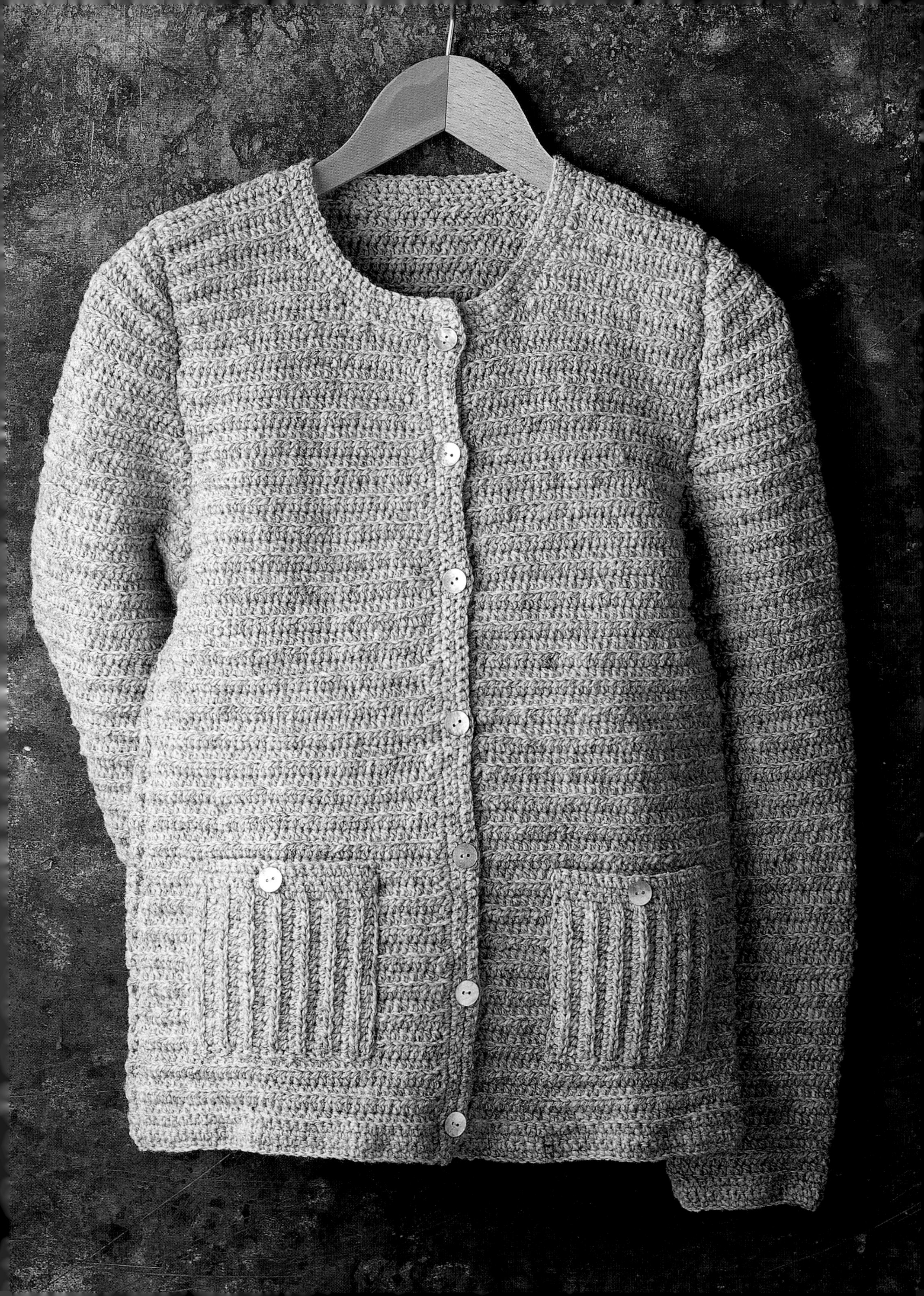

Rep from * to *. **Next row:** ** Work 1 sl st in next st, cont in ribbed sc to end of row, turn the work **. Rep from ** to ** = 33 (36) sts. Cont straight in ribbed sc until right front measures 19-$\frac{1}{2}$ (20) in [50 (51) cm] from base chain. **Neck and shoulders:** Next row: With rs facing, work 1 sl st in each of next 8 sts, cont in ribbed sc to end of row. Work 1 row straight. **Next row:** With rs facing, work 1 sl st in each of next 3 sts, cont in ribbed sc to end of row = 22 (25) sts. Cont straight in ribbed sc until right front measures 21-$\frac{1}{4}$ (21-$\frac{3}{4}$) in [54 (55) cm] from base chain. **Next row:** * With ws facing, work 1 sc into each of next 9 (10) sts, cont to end of row. Work 1 row straight *. Rep from * to * = 4 (5) sts. Fasten off.

Left front: Work as given for right, reversing the armhole, neck and shoulder shaping.

SLEEVES (MAKE 2)

Work 61 (65) ch sts for a base chain, then work 4 rows as follows: 1 ch, then 1 sc over each st of preceding row.

Row 5: Continue in ribbed sc (working through back strand only of each st in preceding row), st over st. Work straight in ribbed sc until sleeve measures 16-$\frac{1}{2}$ (17) in. **Shoulder cap: Next row:** * Work 1 sl st in each of next 3 sts, cont in ribbed sc until 3 sts remain, turn the work *, rep from * to * once. **Next row:** ** Work 1 sl st in each of next 2 sts, cont in ribbed sc until 2 sts remain, turn the work **, rep from ** to ** 4 times. **Next row:** ° Work 1 sl st in next st, cont in ribbed sc until 1 st remains, turn the work °, rep from ° to ° 6 times = 15 (17) sts. Cont straight in ribbed sc until sleeve measures 23-$\frac{1}{2}$ (24) in [60 (61) cm] from base chain. Fasten off.

ASSEMBLY

Darn in all the yarn ends.
Place fronts and back with rs tog. Backstitch the shoulder seams. Fit a shoulder cap into each armhole, then backstitch the armhole, side and sleeve seams.

FINISHING

Rejoin the yarn with a sl st at right front neck edge with rs facing. Work 23 sc across right front ending at shoulder seam, 29 sc across the back, and 23 sc from left shoulder seam to left neck edge = 75 sts. Work in sc for 4 rows. Fasten off.
(pattern continued on page 218)

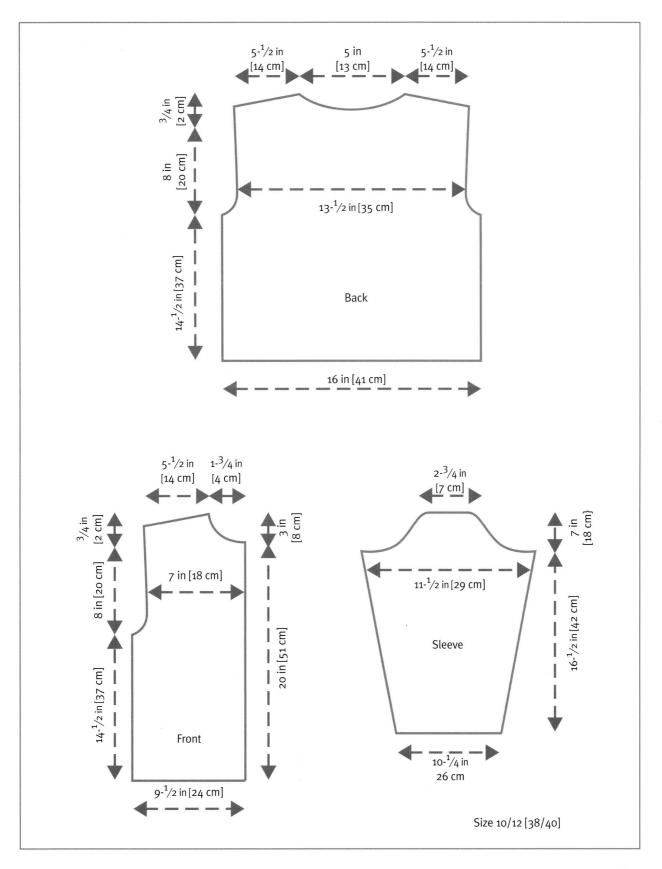

5-1/2 in [14 cm]   5 in [13 cm]   5-1/2 in [14 cm]

3/4 in [2 cm]

8 in [20 cm]

13-1/2 in [35 cm]

14-1/2 in [37 cm]

Back

16 in [41 cm]

5-1/2 in [14 cm]   1-3/4 in [4 cm]

2-3/4 in [7 cm]

3/4 in [2 cm]

3 in [8 cm]

7 in [18 cm]

8 in [20 cm]

11-1/2 in [29 cm]

7 in [18 cm]

20 in [51 cm]

14-1/2 in [37 cm]

Sleeve

16-1/2 in [42 cm]

Front

9-1/2 in [24 cm]

10-1/4 in 26 cm

Size 10/12 [38/40]

83

Scarf and beret

SCARF AND BERET

Materials

For each pattern, 3 50g balls of Rowan "Scottish Tweed" 4-ply yarn (100% wool)

GF Lewis Grey, GM Storm Grey, and GC Grey Mist.

1 3.5 mm crochet hook

1 darning or tapestry needle

1 crewel needle

$^2/_3$ yard [60 cm] 2-in wide grosgrain ribbon (hat-band)

gray sewing thread

pins

Sizes

The finished beret measures approximately 10 in [26 cm] in diameter (one size fits all)

The completed scarf measures 51 X 8-$^3/_4$ in [130 X 22 cm]

Stitches used

Chevrons in single crochet (p.54)

Chevrons in double crochet (p.54)

Double crochet (p. 49)

Single crochet (p. 47)

Skill level

* Beginner (scarf)

*** Experienced (beret)

TO MAKE

BERET

The beret is worked flat, with a series of increases and decreases to give it shape. You will form the final beret shape when you sew the edges together. Begin with the base chain, which is the part that goes around the head.

Using GM Storm Grey, work 122 ch sts for the base chain.

Rows 1–4: Work 1 ch, then cont in sc (st over st).

Row 5: Using GM Storm Grey, 1 ch, * I sc over each of next 10 sc, 2 sc in foll sc *, rep from * to * to end = 133 sts.

Rows 6–7: Using GF Lewis Grey, work chevrons in sc as follows:1 ch, 2 sc over 2nd ch st from hook, * work 1 sc in each of the next 4 ch sts, skip 2 ch sts, 1 sc in each of the foll 4 ch sts, 3 sc in foll ch st *, rep from * to * across the row. End the row by working 2 sc over the last ch st.

Row 7: 1 ch, 2 sc in 1st st of row, then work * 1 sc in each of the next 4 sts, skip 2 sc, 1 sc in each of the next 4 sts, 3 sc in foll st *, rep from * to * across the row. End the row by working 2 sc over the last ch st.

Row 8: Using GC Grey Mist, 1 ch, then work * 1 sc in each of the next 4 sts, skip 2 sc, 1 sc in each of the next 4 sts, 5 sc in foll st *, rep from * to * across the row. End the row by working 3 sc over the last ch st.

Row 9: Using GC Grey Mist, 1 ch, then work * 1 sc in each of the next 5 sts, skip 2 sc, 1 sc in each of the next 5 sts, 3 sc in foll st *, rep from * to * across the row.

Row 10: Using GM Storm Grey, 1 ch, then work * 1 sc in each of the next 5 sts, skip 2 sc, 1 sc in each of the next 5 sts, 5 sc in foll st *, rep from * to * across the row.

Row 11: Using GM Storm Grey, 1 ch, then work * 1 sc in each of the next 6 sts, skip 2 sc, 1 sc in each of the next 6 sts, 3 sc in foll st *, rep from * to * across the row.

Row 12: Using GF Lewis Grey, 1 ch, 2 sc in first st of row, then work * 1 sc in each of the next 6 sts, skip 2 sc, 1 sc in each of the next 6 sts, 5 sc in foll st *, rep from * to * across the row. End with 3 sc in last st of row.

Row 13: Using GF Lewis Grey, 1 ch, then work * 1 sc in each of the next 7 sts, skip 2 sc, 1 sc in each of the next 7 sts, 3 sc in foll st *, rep from * to * across the row.

Row 14: Using GC Grey Mist, 1 ch, then work * 1 sc in each of the next 7 sts, skip 2 sc, 1 sc in each of the next 7 sts, 5 sc in foll st *, rep from * to * across the row. End with 3 sc in last st of row.

Row 15: Using GC Grey Mist, 1 ch, then work * 1 sc in each of the next 8 sts, skip 2 sc, 1 sc in each of the next 8 sts, 3 sc in foll st *, rep from * to * across the row.

Row 16: Using GM Storm Grey, 1 ch, then work * 1 sc in each of the next 8 sts, skip 2 sc, 1 sc in each of the next 8 sts, 5 sc in foll st *, rep from * to * across the row. End with 3 sc in last st of row.

Row 17: Using GM Storm Grey, 1 ch, then work * 1 sc in each of the next 9 sts, skip 2 sc, 1 sc in each of the next 9 sts, 5 sc in foll st *, rep from * to * across the row.

Row 18: Using GF Lewis Grey, 1 ch, then work * 1 sc in each of the next 10 sts, skip 2 sc, 1 sc in each of the next 10 sts, 3 sc in foll st *, rep from * to * across the row. End with 3 sc in last st of row.

Row 19: Using GF Lewis Grey, 1 ch, then work * 1 sc in each of the next 10 sts, skip 2 sc, 1 sc in each of the next 10 sts, 3 sc in foll st *, rep from * to * across the row. End with 3 sc in last st of row.

Rows 20–21: Using GC Grey Mist, 1 ch, then work * 1 sc in each of the next 10 sts, skip 2 sc, 1 sc in each of the next 10 sts, 3 sc in foll st *, rep from * to * across the row. End with 3 sc in last st of row.

Rows 22–23: Using GM Storm Grey, 1 ch, then work * 1 sc in each of the next 10 sts, skip 2 sc, 1 sc in each of the next 10 sts, 3 sc in foll st *, rep from * to * across the row. End with 3 sc in last st of row.

Row 24: Using GF Lewis Grey, 1 ch, 2 sc in first st of row, then * skip 1 st, work 1 sc in each of the next 8 sts, skip 2 sc, 1 sc in each of the next 8 sts, skip 1 st, 3 sc in foll st *, rep from * to * across the row.

Row 25: Using GF Lewis Grey, 1 ch, then work * 1 sc in each of the next 8 sts, skip 2 sc, 1 sc in each of the next 8 sts, 3 sc in foll st *, rep from * to * across the row.

Row 26: Using GC Grey Mist, 1 ch, 2 sc in first st of row, then * skip 1 st, work 1 sc in each of the next 7 sts, skip 2 sc, 1 sc in each of the next 7 sts, skip 1 st, 3 sc in foll st *, rep from * to * across the row.

Row 27: Using GC Grey Mist, 1 ch, then work * 1 sc in each of the next 7 sts, skip 2 sc, 1 sc in each of the next 7 sts, 3 sc in foll st *, rep from * to * across the row.

Row 28: Using GM Storm Grey, 1 ch, 2 sc in first st of row, then * skip 1 st, work 1 sc in each of the next 6 sts, skip 2 sc, 1 sc in each of the next 6 sts, skip 1 st, 3 sc in foll st *, rep from * to * across the row.

Row 29: Using GM Storm Grey, 1 ch, then work * 1 sc in each of the next 6 sts, skip 2 sc, 1 sc in each of the next 6 sts, 3 sc in foll st *, rep from * to * across the row.

Row 30: Using GF Lewis Grey, 1 ch, 2 sc in first st of row, then * skip 1 st, work 1 sc in each of the next 5 sts, skip 2 sc, 1 sc in each of the next 5 sts, skip 1 st, 3 sc in foll st *, rep from * to * across the row.

Row 31: Using GF Lewis Grey, 1 ch, then work * 1 sc in each of the next 5 sts, skip 2 sc, 1 sc in each of the next 5 sts, 3 sc in foll st *, rep from * to * across the row.

Row 32: Using GC Grey Mist, 1 ch, 2 sc in first st of row, then * skip 1 st, work 1 sc in each of the next 4 sts, skip 2 sc, 1 sc in each of the next 4 sts, skip 1 st, 3 sc in foll st *, rep from * to * across the row.

Row 33: Using GC Grey Mist, 1 ch, 2 sc in 1st st of row, then work * 1 sc in each of the next 4 sts, skip 2 sc, 1 sc in each of the next 4 sts, 3 sc in foll st *, rep from * to * across the row. End the row by working 2 sc over the last ch st.

Row 34: Using GM Storm Grey, 1 ch, 2 sc in first st of row, then * skip 1 st, work 1 sc in each of the next 3 sts, skip 2 sc, 1 sc in each of the next 3 sts, skip 1 st, 3 sc in foll st *, rep from * to * across the row.

Row 35: Using GM Storm Grey, continue the chevron, working 3 sc on each side.

Row 36: Using GF Lewis Grey, 1 ch, 2 sc in first st of row, then * skip 1 st, work 1 sc in each of the next 2 sts, skip 2 sc, 1 sc in each of the next 2 sts, skip 1 st, 3 sc in foll st *, rep from * to * across the row.

Row 37: Using GF Lewis Grey, continue the chevron, working 2 sc on each side.

Row 38: Using GC Grey Mist, 1 ch, 2 sc in first st of row, then * skip 1 st, work 1 sc in each of the next 7 sts, skip 2 sc, 1 sc in each of the next 7 sts, skip 1 st, 3 sc in foll st *, rep from * to * across the row.

Row 39: Using GC Grey Mist, 1 ch, then 1 sc in each st across the row.

Rows 40–41: Using GM Storm Grey, 1 ch, then * work 1 sc in each of the next 2 sts, skip 1 st *, rep from * to * across the row.

Rows 42–43: Using GF Lewis Grey, 1 ch, then * work 1 sc in each of the next 2 sts, skip 1 st *, rep from * to * across the row until 4 sts remain. Fasten off.

ASSEMBLY

Close up the beret as follows: Fold the work in half rs tog and backstitch the sides.

Using the thread and the crewel needle, hemstitch the grosgrain ribbon to the inside edge along the base chain.

SCARF

Using GM Storm Grey, work 56 ch sts for a base chain.

Work the entire scarf in chevrons in double crochet, switching the color every 2 rows. Cont in pattern until scarf measures 51 in [130 cm] from base chain. Fasten off.

462

8402

3

TEXTURED STITCHES

Too long ignored, textured stitches are much less complicated than they appear. By winding the yarn around the hook a few times, or working sideways through the stitches, you can rapidly build textures that have striking three-dimensional effects. Some raised crochet stitches look similar to Aran patterns, which are traditionally knit on needles. You'll soon develop the skill required for these stitches: All you have to do is work a sample swatch or two before you start your pattern.

Raised stitches

HORIZONTAL RIBBING

There are two main types of raised stitch. The first is the ribbing family: horizontal or vertical. The second type is worked by combining groups of stitches to obtain a particular surface texture.

1. To form horizontal ribbing, insert the hook under a single strand at the top of a stitch in the preceding row or round.

2. Work the stitch.

3. The second strand of the stitch you worked into forms a horizontal bar. As you continue row upon row, the horizontal ribbing takes on the appearance of a woven fabric. Work horizontal ribbing under the back or front strand of the stitches in the preceding row according to the instructions for the pattern you're following.

 →  →

VERTICAL RIBBING

Vertical ribbing forms as you bring the hook around the stem (the vertical strands) of a stitch in the preceding row. This type of stitch is most often worked over a base of double crochets

RAISED DOUBLE CROCHET IN FRONT OF WORK

1. Yo, insert hook from front to back and from right to left around the vertical strands of a st in the preceding row.

2. Work the loops off the hook 2 by 2.

RAISED DOUBLE CROCHET AT BACK OF WORK

1. Yo, insert hook from back to front and from right to left around the vertical strands of a st in the preceding row.

2. Work the loops off the hook 2 by 2.

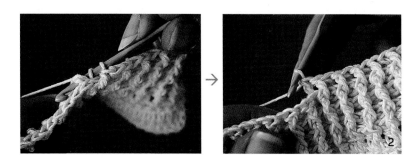

CLUSTERS

CLUSTER FORMED OF 3 DOUBLE CROCHETS

1. Work 1 dc into a stitch, leaving last lp of dc on hook.

2. Work another dc into same st as before, leaving last lp of dc on hook.

3. Work a third dc into same st, leaving last lp of dc on hook = 4 lps on hook.

4. Yo and draw through all 4 lps on hook.

5. The resulting stitch forms a "popcorn" cluster. When you work a cluster with more than 5 dc, you may sometimes have to work an extra ch st to maintain the raised effect.

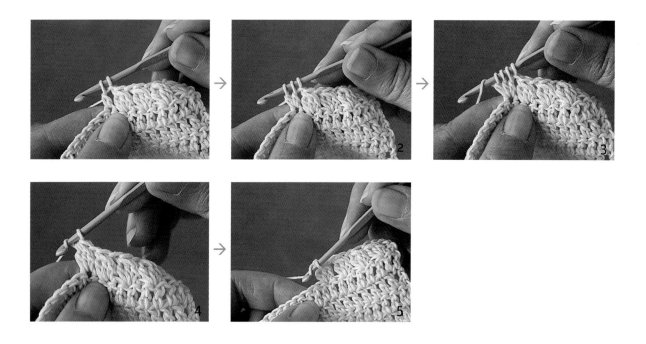

PUFF STITCHES

Puff stitches are similar to clusters, but are worked a little differently. The basic stitch for a puff stitch is the half-double crochet.

A PUFF STITCH FORMED OF 3 HALF-DC

1. Yo, insert hook in st of previous row, yo again.

2. * Draw up a slightly extended loop *: you now have 3 lps on the hook.

3–4. Repeat steps 1–2 twice more, working into the same st of the previous row = 8 lps on hook.

5. Yo and draw lp through all lps on hook.

6. Finish off by working 1 ch to keep the puff st raised.

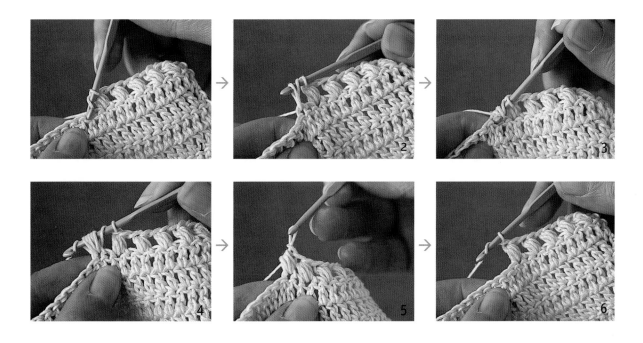

CROSSED DOUBLE CROCHETS

Crossed double crochets are used for a number of open-work or eyelet patterns.

1. Yo twice, insert hook in a st of preceding row.

2. Draw up lp, yo and draw lp through 2 lps, leaving 3 lps on hook.

3. Yo, skip a st, insert hook in foll st.

4. Draw up a lp, yo and draw through 2 lps on hook. Yo and draw through 2 lps on hook = 3 lps remain on hook.

Now yo and draw through 2 loops on hook, yo and draw lp through 2 lps = 1 st remains.

5. Work 1 ch st, yo, insert hook under both upper strands where preceding double crochets cross.

6. Draw up a lp, yo and draw through 2 lps, yo and draw through remaining 2 lps.

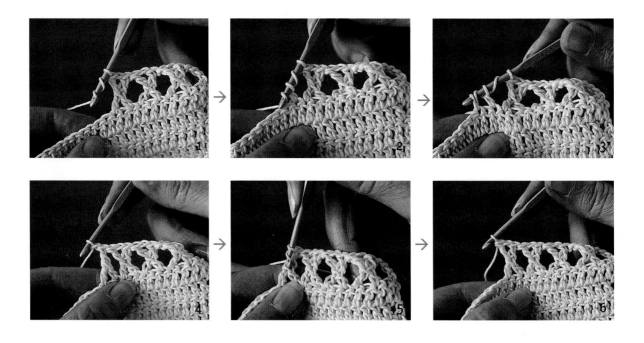

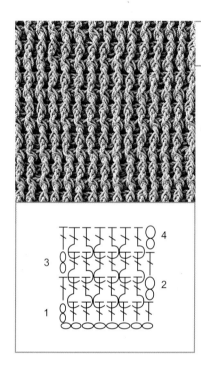

VERTICAL RIBBING

Work a base chain with chain stitches in a multiple of 2 sts plus 2.

Row 1 (ws of work): 3 ch (to count as first dc of row), 1 dc in st of base chain.

Row 2 (rs of work): 2 ch (to count as first dc), skip 1 st, * 1 raised dc through front strand of next dc, 1 raised dc through back strand of foll dc *, rep from * to * across the row. End by working 1 dc over 3rd ch st at beg of previous row.

Following rows: Rep Row 2.

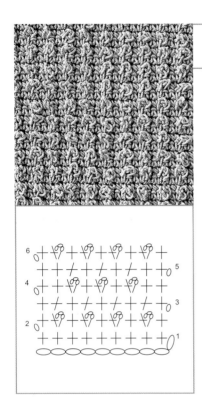

GRANULAR STITCH

Work a base chain with a multiple of 4 stitches plus 1 stitch.

Row 1 (rs of work): 1 sc in 2nd st from hook, 1 sc in each st of base chain.

Row 2 (ws of work): 1 ch, 1 sc in first st, * 1 granular sc (gsc as follows: with ws facing, insert hook in next st, yo and draw up lp, [yo and work 1 st off hook] 3 times, thus forming 3 ch sts, yo and slip off remaining 2 lps. Pull each "grain" to rs of work), 1 sc over foll st *, rep from * to * across the row.

Row 3: 1 ch, 1 sc over first st of row, 1 sc in each foll st of row.

Row 4: 1 ch, 1 sc in first st of row, 1 sc in foll st, * 1 gsc in next st, 1 sc in foll st*, rep from * to * across the row. end with 1 sc in last st of row.

Following rows: Rep Rows 1–4.

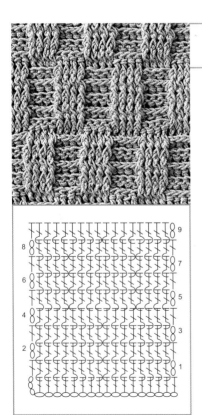

BASKET WEAVE

Work a base chain with a multiple of 8 stitches plus 2 stitches.

Base row (ws of work): 3 ch (to count as first dc of row), 1 dc in each foll st of base chain.

Row 1 (rs of work): 2 ch (to count as first dc of row), skip 1 st, * work 1 raised dc through front strand only of each of next 4 sts, work 1 raised dc through back strand only of each of foll 4 sts *, rep from * to *. End with 1 dc in last ch st of previous row.

Rows 2–4: Rep Row 1.

Row 5: 2 ch (to count as first dc), skip 1 st, * 1 raised dc through back strand only of each of next 4 sts, 1 raised dc through front strand only of each of next 4 sts *, rep from * to *. End the row with 1 dc in last ch st of previous row.

Rows 6–8: Rep Row 5.

Following rows: Rep Rows 1–8.

HONEYCOMB STITCH

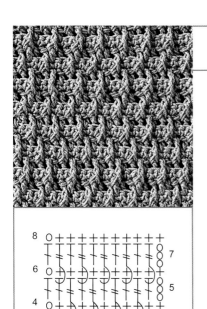

Work a base chain with a multiple of 2 stitches plus 1 stitch.

Row 1 (rs of work): 3 ch (to count as first dc of row), 1 dc in each st of base chain.

Row 2 and all even-numbered rows (ws): 1 ch (= first dc of row), 1 sc in each st of previous row.

Row 3: 3 ch (to count as first dc), skip first st, * 1 tr through front strand only of dc below next sc, 1 dc in foll st *, rep from * to *. End with 1 dc over last st.

Row 5: 3 ch (to count as first dc), skip first st, * 1 dc in next st, 1 tr through front strand only of dc below next sc *, rep from * to *. End with 1 dc in each of last 2 sts of row.

Following rows: Rep Rows 2–5.

RAISED PETALS

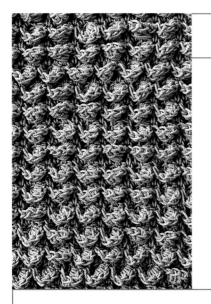

Work a base chain with a multiple of 3 stitches plus 1 stitch.

Row 1 (ws of work): 3 ch (to count as first dc of row), 1 dc in each ch st of base chain.

Row 2 (rs of work): Do not work 1 ch to turn, work 1 group of petals (gp = 1 sc, 1 half-dc, 3 dc) around the stem of the first dc, skip 2 sts, 1 sl st in top of next dc, * 1 gp around same dc as sl st last worked, skip 2 sts, 1 sl st in top of foll dc *, rep from * to *. End with a sl st in last st.

Note: This row is worked at the same length as the sts in the previous row. Row 2 adds a raised texture, but does not increase the length of the stitches.

Row 3: 3 ch (to count as first dc), skip 1 st, work 1 dc in each st of previous row.

Following rows: Repeat Rows 2 and 3.

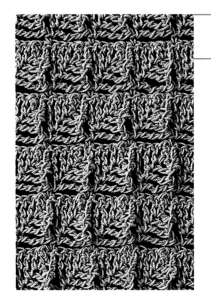

TRIANGULAR LEAVES

Work a base chain with a multiple of 6 stitches plus 1 stitch.

Row 1 (ws of work): 1 ch, 1 sc in 2nd st from hook, * 1 triangular bar (tb: work 6 ch, 1 sc in 2nd ch st from hook, 1 tr in foll ch st, 1 dc in next ch st, 1 tr in foll ch st, 1 dbl tr in foll st), skip 5 sts of the base chain, work 1 sc in foll ch st *, rep from * to * across the row. End with 1 sc.

Row 2 (rs of work): 5 ch (to count as first dbl tr of row), * 1 sc at top of tb, down other side of tb work 1 sc in next ch st, 1 tr in foll ch st, 1 dc in next ch st, 1 tr in foll ch st, and 1 dbl tr in next ch st *. Rep from * to * across the row. Close the final tb by replacing the last dbl tr with ** yo 3 times, insert hook in last ch st of final tb, yo and draw up lp, then work (yo and through 2 lps on hook) 3 times **. Rep from ** to ** in last sc, yo one more time, and work off the remaining 3 lps from the hook.

Row 3: 1 ch, 1 sc in first st, * 1 tb, skip the next 5 sts, 1 sc in foll st *, rep from * to * across the row. End the row with 1 sc in the 5th of 5 ch sts of previous row.

Following rows: Repeat Rows 2–3.

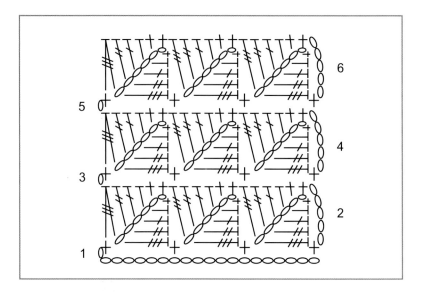

RAISED CHEVRONS

Work a base chain with a multiple of 16 stitches plus 1 stitch.

Row 1: 3 ch (to count as first dc, 2 dc tog over the next 2 ch sts (= 3 dc tog altogether), * 1 dc in each of the next 5 ch sts, work (2 dc, 1 ch, 2 dc) in foll ch st, 1 dc in each of the next 5 ch sts, 5 dc tog over foll 5 ch sts *. Rep from * to * across the row. End the row by working 3 dc tog over the last 3 ch sts of the row.

Row 2: 3 ch (to count as first dc), skip first st, work 2 dc through back strand only of each of next 2 sts (= 3 raised dc altogether), * 1 dc through front strand only of each of next 5 sts, in next st work (2 dc, 1 ch, 1 dc), then 1 dc through front strand only of each of next 5 sts, now over next 5 sts work tog 5 dc through back strand only *. Rep from * to * across the row. End with 3 dc tog over the last 3 sts.

Row 3: 3 ch, skip 1 st, now under the next 2 sts work 2 dc tog through front strand only (counts as 3 raised dc tog), work 1 dc through back strand only of next 5 sts, (2 dc, 1 ch, 2 dc) in foll ch st, 1 dc through back strand only of next 5 sts, 1 dc through front strand only of foll 5 sts *. Rep from * to * across the row. End by working 3 dc tog through front strand only of last 3 sts.

Following rows: Repeat Rows 2 and 3.

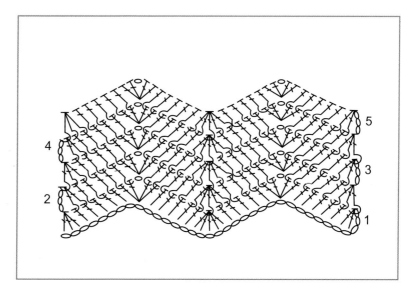

CHEVRONS AND PUFF STITCHES

Work a base chain with a multiple of 17 stitches.

Row 1: 3 ch, 1 dc in next ch st (counts as 2 dc tog), now work 2 dc tog over foll 2 ch sts) twice, * (1 ch, 1 puff st in foll ch st) 5 times, 1 ch, (2 dc tog over next 2 ch sts) 6 times *, rep from * to * across the row. End by working (2 dc tog over next 2 ch sts) 3 times.

Row 2: 1 ch, 1 sc in first st, then 1 sc in each foll st of row.

Row 3: 3 ch, skip 1 st, work 1 dc in foll st (= 2 dc tog), now work (2 dc tog over next 2 sts) twice, * (1 ch, 1 puff st in foll st) 5 times, 1 ch, (2 dc tog over foll 2 sts) 6 times *, rep from * to * across the row. End by working (2 dc tog over next 2 sts) 3 times.

Following rows: Repeat Rows 2 and 3.

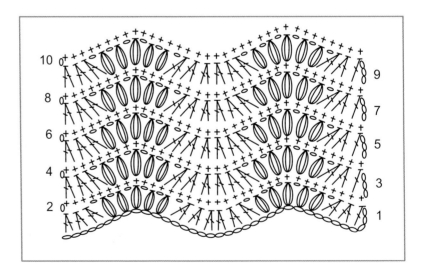

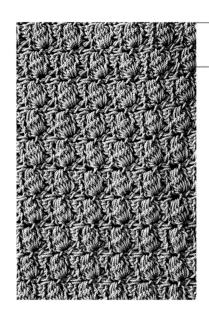

CORNCOB STITCH

Work a base chain with a multiple of 4 stitches plus 1 stitch.

Row 1 (rs of work): 1 ch, 1 sc in 2nd st from hook, * 3 ch, 1 corn st (= a puff st formed of 5 dc) over the same ch st as the preceding sc, skip 3 ch sts, work 1 sc in foll ch st *, rep from * to * across the row. End with 1 sc in last st.

Row 2: 3 ch (to count as first dc), skip first st, work * 1 sc in each of next 2 ch sts, 1 half-dc in foll ch st, 1 dc in next sc *, rep from * to *. End by working 1 dc over last st.

Row 3: 1 ch, work 1 sc in first st, * 3 ch, 1 corn st over same st as preceding sc, 1 sc over next dc *, rep from * to *. End with 1 sc over 3rd ch st of preceding row.

Following rows: Repeat Rows 2 and 3.

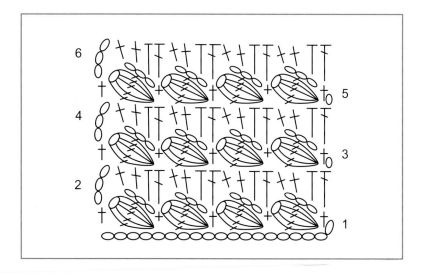

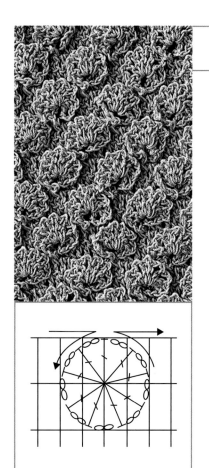

ROSETTES

Work a base chain with a multiple of 8 stitches plus 5 stitches.

Row 1 (rs of work): 3 ch (to cont as first dc), work 1 dc in 4th st from hook, then 1 dc in each ch st of base chain.

Row 2: 3 ch (to count as first dc), skip 1 st, work 1 dc in each of next 3 sts, * 1 rosette (work [1 dc, 2 ch] 9 times into the same st, slightly extend the loop on the hook and withdraw the hook then reinsert it from ws to rs through the top of the first dc of rosette, keeping the sts at the back of the work. Pick up the dropped st and draw it through the loop on the hook) over next st, 1 dc in each of foll 7 sts *, rep from * to * across the row. End by working 1 dc in the 3rd ch st of previous row.

Row 3: 3 ch (to count as first dc), skip 1 st, work 1 dc in each st of previous row. End by working 1 dc in 3rd ch st of previous row.

Row 4: 3 ch (to count as first dc), skip 1 st, * 1 dc in each of next 7 sts, 1 rosette st in foll st *, rep from * to * across the row. End by working 1 dc in 3rd ch st of previous row.

Row 5: Rep Row 3.

Following rows: Repeat Rows 2–5.

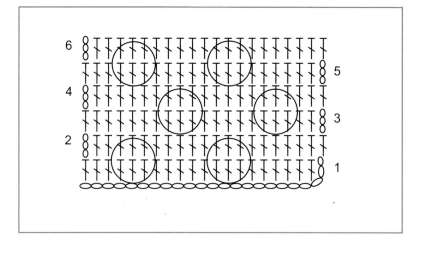

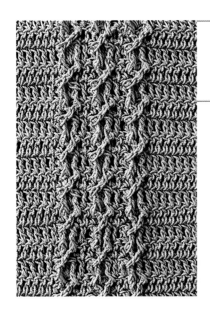

PUFF STITCHES OVER CROSSED DOUBLE CROCHETS

The raised pattern is worked over 11 sts on top of a background of any number of stitches.

Row 1 (rs of work): 3 ch (to count as first dc), work 1 dc over 4th st from hook, then 1 dc in each st of the previous row.

Row 2: Beg the row with dc for the background, then form the pattern as follows: work (1 tr through back strand only of st in preceding row, 1 puff st formed of 5 half-dc in foll st, 1 tr through back strand only of st in previous row, 1 dc) 3 times, and cont the background in dc.

Row 3: Work the following incomplete sts, leaving the last loop of each st on the hook * (1 dc in next st, skip the puff st , work 1 tr through front strand only under next st), yo and work 3 loops off hook at once, work 1 dc over foll puff st, then leaving the last lp of each st on hook work (1 tr through front strand only under st of same puff st as before, 1 dc in foll st of puff st), yo and draw lp through all 3 lps on hook, 1 dc *. Rep from * to * twice. Cont the background in dc.

Row 4: Beg the row with dc for the background, then form the pattern as follows: work (1 tr through back strand only of raised st in preceding row, 1 puff st formed of 5 half-dc in foll st, 1 tr through back strand only of raised st in previous row, 1 dc) 3 times, and cont the background in dc.

Following rows: Repeat Rows 3 and 4.

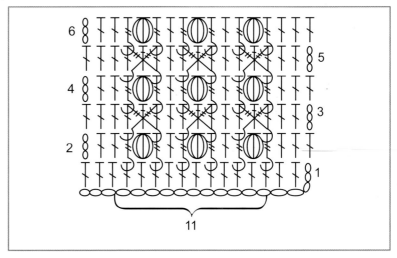

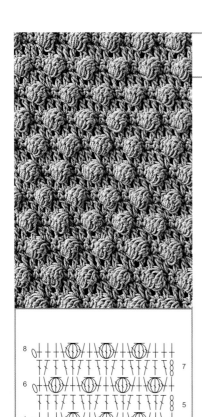

STAGGERED CLUSTER STITCHES

Work a base chain with a multiple of 4 stitches plus 1 stitch.

Row 1 (rs of work): 3 ch (to count as first dc), work 1 dc over 4th st from hook, then cont with 1 dc in each st of previous row.

Row 2: 1 ch, 1 sc in each of next 2 sts, * 1 cluster st formed of 5 dc in foll st, 1 sc in each of next 3 sts *, rep from * to * across the row. End with 1 sc over each of the last 2 sts of the row.

Row 3: 3 ch (to count as first dc), skip 1 st, work 1 dc in each st of previous row.

Row 4: 1 ch, 1 sc in each of the next 4 sts, * 1 cluster in foll st, 1 sc in each of the next 3 sts *, rep from * to * across the row. End with 1 sc in each of the last 4 sts.

Row 5: Repeat Row 3.

Following rows: Repeat Rows 2–5.

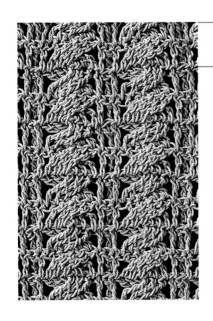

RAISED CABLES

The raised cable pattern is worked over 19 sts on top of a background of any number of double crochet stitches.

Row 1 (rs of work): Work the background in dc, then for the raised cables, work 1 tr through front strand only of next st in previous row, work 1 dc over foll st, skip next 3 sts, work 1 dbl tr in each of the next 3 sts, then bringing the hook behind the preceding 3 dbl tr work 1 dbl tr in each of the 3 skipped sts, continue with 1 dc in next st, 1 tr through front strand only of next st, 1 dc in foll st, skip the next 3 sts, work 1 dbl tr in each of the next 3 sts, then bringing the hook in front of the preceding 3 dbl tr work 1 dbl tr in each of the 3 skipped sts, 1 dc in next st, 1 tr through front strand only of foll st.

Row 2: Beg with dc for the background, then over the sts for the cable pattern work 1 tr through back strand only of next st, 1 dc over foll st, skip 3 sts, work 1 dbl tr in each of the foll 3 sts, bringing the hook behind the preceding 3 dbl tr work 1 dbl tr in each of the 3 skipped sts, work 1 dc in the foll st, 1 tr through front strand only of next st, 1 dc in foll st, skip 3 sts, work 1 dbl tr in each of the next 3 sts, then bringing the hook in front of the preceding 3 dbl tr work 1 dbl tr in each of the 3 skipped sts, 1 dc in foll st, 1 tr through back strand only of foll st.

Following rows: Repeat Rows 1 and 2.

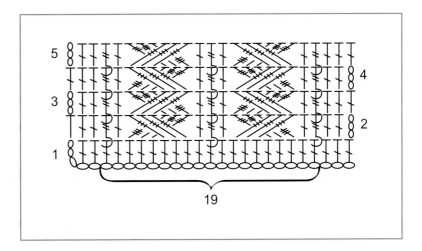

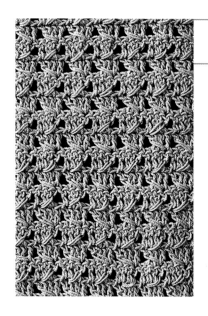

MARY QUITE CONTRARY STITCH

Work a base chain with a multiple of 4 stitches plus 2 stitches.

Row 1: 3 ch (to count as first dc), then into 4th st from hook work * 1 dc, followed by 1 dc in each of the next 3 sts, skip foll ch st and work 1 diagonal dc (see chart) *, rep from * to * across the row. End by working 1 dc over the 3rd ch st at beg of previous row.

Row 2: 3 ch (to count as first dc), skip 1 st, *1 dc over each of the next 3 sts, skip 1 st, work 1 diagonal dc *, rep from * to * across the row. End by working 1 dc over the 3rd ch st at beg of previous row.

Following rows: Repeat Row 2.

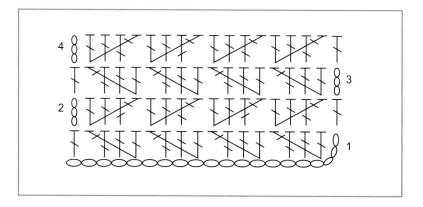

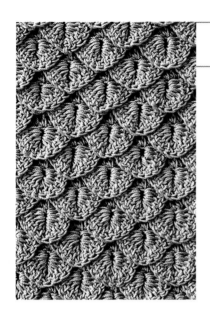

RAISED SCALES

Work a base chain with a multiple of 10 stitches plus 2 stitches.

Row 1 (ws of work): 3 ch (to count as first dc), work 1 dc in 4th st from hook, then 1 dc over each st of the preceding row.

Row 2: 1 ch (to count as first sc of row), skip 1 dc, work 1 sc bet 2 dc, * skip 4 sts, work 6 dc bringing the hook from right to left under the foll dc and working the length of this dc (see chart), now work 6 dc bringing the hook from left to right under the foll dc and working up the length of this dc, skip 4 sts, work 1 dc bet 2 dc *. Rep from * to * across the row. End by skipping 1 dc and working 1 dc in the last dc.

Row 3: Repeat Row 1.

Row 4: 1 ch (to count as first sc), under the next dc work 6 dc bringing the hook from right to left and working down the length of this dc, then work 6 dc bringing the hook from left to right under the next dc and working up the length of this dc, * skip 4 sts, work 1 sc bet 2 dc, skip 4 sts, under the next dc work 6 dc bringing the hook from right to left and working down the length of this dc, then work 6 dc bringing the hook from left to right and working up the length of this dc *. Repeat from * to * across the row. End by working 1 sc in the last dc.

Following rows: Repeat Rows 2, 3, and 4.

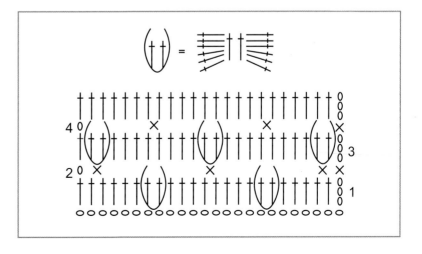

Square pillow

SQUARE PILLOW

Materials

3 50g balls of Rowan
"Scottish Tweed"
(100% wool)

Apple

1 4 mm crochet hook

Lining: Natural linen fabric
measuring 25-1/2 X 55 in
[65 X 140 cm].

Green and natural sewing
threads

1 darning needle

1 crewel needle

pins

A pillow form measuring 16
in [40 cm] square

A ruler

A fine-point indelible marker

Size

Finished pillow measures
approximately
24 X 24 in [60 X 60 cm]

Stitches used

Vertical ribbing (p. 95)

Triangular leaves (p. 98)

Skill level

* Beginner

TO MAKE

To complete the cushion, work 2 squares in vertical ribbing and 2 squares in triangular leaves.

SQUARE IN VERTICAL RIBBING

Work 43 ch sts for a base chain and follow the directions on p. 95 to complete 23 rows in vertical ribbing. At the completion of Row 23, fasten off. Complete a second identical square.

SQUARE IN TRIANGULAR LEAVES

Work 36 ch sts for a base chain and follow the directions on p. 98 to work triangular leaves over 7 motifs across the row for 6 rows. On completing the 42 motifs, fasten off. Complete a second, identical square.

ASSEMBLY

1. Darn in all the yarn ends.

2. Place 2 squares (1 vertical ribbing, 1 triangular leaves) rs tog. Join the squares by backstitching along one side. Join the other 2 squares in the same way. Place the 2 rectangles thus formed rs tog, making sure that you have the squares in contrasting positions, and backstitch the seam to make a square approximately 16 in [40 cm] on a side.

PILLOW SLIP

On the ws of the linen fabric, using the marker and the ruler, draw one 24 in [60 cm] square and 2 rectangles each measuring 24 X 18-1/2 in [60 X 47 cm]. Cut out the pieces, allowing a 5/8 in [1/5 cm] seam allowance outside the ruled lines.

Overcast the edges to prevent fraying. Use a hot iron to press 3/4 in [2 cm] to the wrong side along one long edge of each rectangle. You now have 2 rectangles measuring 24 X 17-1/2 [60 X 45 cm].

Place the crocheted square and the 2 rectangles rs tog, placing the

hems together at the center (see chart). Pin the pieces in position then slipstitch along the ruled lines. Trim the corners with pinking shears, press the seams open, and turn the pillow right side out.

Press the seam allowances flat. Over the square for the top of the slip, draw a line 3 in [8 cm] from each edge, making a 16-in [40-cm] square. Stitch by hand or machine along this line through all thicknesses of the pillow.

Pin the crocheted square over the top of the slip, aligning the edges with the row of stitching on the slip.

Using the green thread slipstitch by hand the crocheted square to the top of the slip. Insert the pillow form in the slip.

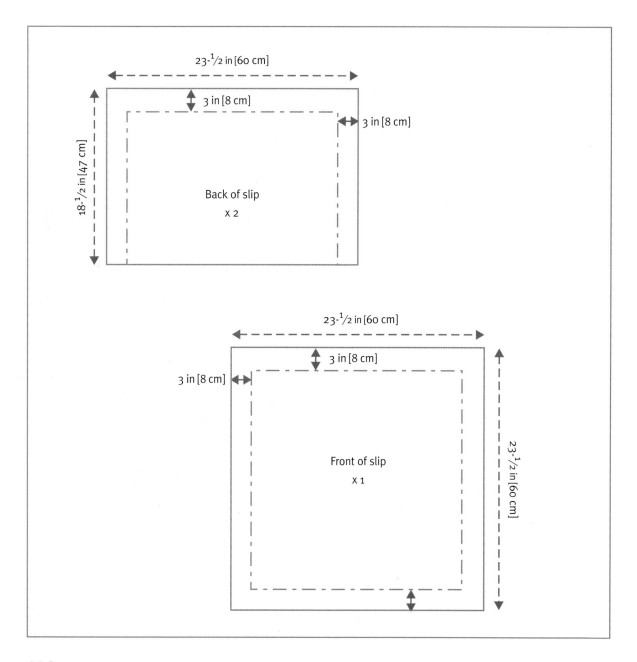

CARRIER BAG

Materials

3 50g balls of Gedifra "Korella" (53% linen, 47% acrylic)

Blue Jean no. 8462

1 3 mm crochet hook

Lining: toning printed fabric measuring 12 X 36 in [30 X 90 cm].

Indigo blue sewing thread

1 darning needle

1 crewel needle

An 8-in [20 cm] zip fastener

Pins

Tailor's chalk

A brown leather handle, 17 in [43 cm] long

A tassel charm

Size

Finished bag measures approximately

7-$\frac{1}{2}$ X 13-$\frac{1}{2}$ X 1-$\frac{1}{4}$ in [19 X 34 X 3 cm] (not including the handle)

Stitches used

Half-double crochet (p. 41)

Raised scales (p. 107)

Skill level

** Some experience

TO MAKE

BODY (MAKE 2)

Work 61 ch sts for a base chain.

Rows 1–2: Work 2 ch, then 1 half-dc in each st of the previous row.

Row 3: 2 ch, 1 half-dc over each of the next 9 sts, skip 1 st, 1 half-dc over each of the next 39 sts, skip 1 st, 1 half-dc over each of the foll 10 sts.

Row 4: 2 ch, 1 half-dc over each of the next 9 sts, skip 1 st, 1 half-dc over each of the next 37 sts, skip 1 st, 1 half-dc over each of the foll 10 sts.

Row 5: 2 ch, 1 half-dc over each of the next 9 sts, skip 1 st, 1 half-dc over each of the next 35 sts, skip 1 st, 1 half-dc over each of the foll 10 sts.

Row 6: 2 ch, 1 half-dc over each of the next 9 sts, skip 1 st, 1 half-dc over each of the next 33 sts, skip 1 st, 1 half-dc over each of the foll 10 sts.

Row 7: 2 ch, 1 half-dc over each of the next 9 sts, skip 1 st, 1 half-dc over each of the next 31 sts, skip 1 st, 1 half-dc over each of the foll 10 sts.

Row 8: 2 ch, 1 half-dc over each of the next 9 sts, skip 1 st, 1 half-dc over each of the next 29 sts, skip 1 st, 1 half-dc over each of the foll 10 sts.

Row 9: 2 ch, 1 half-dc over each of the next 9 sts, skip 1 st, 1 half-dc over each of the next 27 sts, skip 1 st, 1 half-dc over each of the foll 10 sts.

Row 10: 2 ch, 1 half-dc over each of the next 9 sts, skip 1 st, 1 half-dc over each of the next 25 sts, skip 1 st, 1 half-dc over each of the foll 10 sts.

Row 11: 2 ch, 1 half-dc over each of the next 9 sts, skip 1 st, 1 half-dc over each of the next 23 sts, skip 1 st, 1 half-dc over each of the foll 10 sts = 43 sts.

Row 12: 3 ch, then work 1 dc over each foll st.

Row 13: Work 4 raised scales as follows: 1 ch (counts as first sc of row), skip 1 dc, work 1 sc bet 2 dc, * skip 4 sts, work 6 dc bringing the hook from right to left under foll dc and working the length of this dc (see chart on p. 107), then work 6 dc bringing the hook from left to right under foll dc and working the length of this dc, skip 4 sts, 1 sc bet 2 dc *. Rep from * to * 3 times across the row. To end the row, skip 1 dc, work 1 sc over final dc.

Row 14: 3 ch, then work 1 dc over each foll st.

Row 15: Work 5 raised scales as follows: 1 ch (counts as first sc of row), work 6 dc bringing the hook from right to left under foll dc and working the length of this dc, then work 6 dc bringing the hook from left to right under foll dc and working the length of this dc, *skip 4 sts, 1 sc bet 2 dc, skip 4 sts, work 6 dc bringing the hook from right to left under foll dc and working the length of this dc, then work 6 dc bringing the hook from left to right under foll dc and working the length of this dc *. Rep from * to * 4 times across the row. To end the row, work 1 sc over final dc.

Row 16: 3 ch, then work 1 dc over each foll st.

Row 17: Work 4 raised scales as follows: 1 ch, skip 1 dc, work 1 sc bet 2 dc, * skip 4 sts, work 6 dc bringing the hook from right to left under foll dc and working the length of this dc, then work 6 dc bringing the hook from left to right under foll dc and working the length of this dc, skip 4 sts, 1 sc bet 2 dc *. Rep from * to * 3 times across the row. To end the row, skip 1 dc, work 1 sc over final dc.

Row 18: 3 ch, then work 1 dc over each foll st.

Row 19: 2 ch, 1 half-dc over each of the next 9 sts, skip 1 st, 1 half-dc over each of the next 21 sts, skip 1 st, 1 half-dc over each of the foll 10 sts.

Row 20: 2 ch, 1 half-dc over each of the next 9 sts, skip 1 st, 1 half-dc over each of the next 19 sts, skip 1 st, 1 half-dc over each of the foll 10 sts.

Row 21: 2 ch, 1 half-dc over each of the next 9 sts, skip 1 st, 1 half-dc over each of the next 17 sts, skip 1 st, 1 half-dc over each of the foll 10 sts.

Row 22: 2 ch, 1 half-dc over each of the next 9 sts, skip 1 st, 1 half-dc over each of the next 15 sts, skip 1 st, 1 half-dc over each of the foll 10 sts.

Row 23: 2 ch, 1 half-dc over each of the next 9 sts, skip 1 st, 1 half-dc over each of the next 13 sts, skip 1 st, 1 half-dc over each of the foll 10 sts. Fasten off.

Complete a second, identical section.

Darn in all the yarn ends.

GUSSET

Work 151 ch sts for a base chain.

Rows 1–5: 2 ch, then 1 dc over each st of previous row. At completion of Row 5, fasten off. Darn in the yarn ends.

ASSEMBLY

Using tailor's chalk, trace the outline of the body twice on the ws of the lining fabric. Cut out the lining pieces, leaving a $3/4$ in [2 cm] seam allowance.

Join the gusset to front and back with a row of sc on the rs of the work as follows: Pin the gusset ws tog around 1 side of the bag, leaving 10 sts free at each end of the gusset. Work 1 row of sc, forming the 2 corners by working 3 sc into same st at each corner.

Join the gusset to the other side in the same way. Darn in all the yarn ends.

Fold the ends of the gusset to the inside through the rings at each end of the leather handle and backstitch in place.

FINISHING

Pin the 2 sections of the lining rs tog and stitch $1/2$ in [1 cm] from the edge. Trim the seam allowance with pinking shears to prevent fraying. Slip the lining into the bag, ws tog.

Pin the zip fastener in place and stitch. Fold $3/4$ in [2 cm] to the inside around the top of the lining. Slipstitch the edge of the lining to the inside of the bag, covering the zipper tape as you go. Attach a tassel charm to the zipper pull.

Irish sweater

IRISH SWEATER

Materials
15 50g balls of Rowan "Cotton Wool" (50% merino wool, 50% cotton)

Moka no. 965

1 3.5 mm crochet hook

1 darning or tapestry needle

Pins

Size
Women's US 8/10—12/14 (EUR 38/40—40/42)

Instructions for the larger size are shown in parentheses. When only one number is given, it applies to both sizes.

Stitches used
Double crochet (p. 42)

Vertical ribbing (p. 95)

Staggered clusters (p. 104)

Honeycomb (p. 97)

Raised cables (p.105)

Skill level
*** Experienced

TO MAKE

BACK
Work 79 (85) ch sts for a base chain.

Row 1: 3 ch (to count as first dc of row), then 1 dc in each st of base chain.

Rows 2–4: Follow the directions on p. 95 to complete these 3 rows in vertical ribbing (= 1-¼ in [3 cm]).

Row 5: 3 ch (= first dc of row), then 1 dc in each st of base chain.

Rows 6–39 (43): Follow the chart on p. 117 and the instructions for honeycomb stitch (p. 97), raised cables (p. 105), and staggered clusters (p.104) to form the pattern. In Rows 14 (16), 20 (22), 26 (28), and 30 (32) follow the instructions on p. 26–28 to inc by 1 st at each end of the row until, in Row 31 (33), you are working with 87 (93) sts. Cont straight in pattern to the end of Row 39 (43).

Armholes: Row 40 (44): Work forward with a sl st in each of the first 3 (4) sts, cont in pattern sts until 3 (4) sts remain; turn the work.

Next row: * Work forward with a sl st in each of the first 2 sts, cont in pattern sts until 2 sts remain; turn the work *. Rep from * to * once.

Next row: ** Work forward with a sl st in the first st, cont in pattern sts until 1 st remains; turn the work *. Rep from * to * twice = 67 (71) sts. Cont straight in pattern to the end of Row 67 (71).

Shoulders: Next row: Work forward with a sl st in each of the first 8 sts, cont in pattern sts until 8 sts remain; turn the work.

Next row: Work forward with a sl st in each of the first 6 sts, cont in pattern sts until 6 sts remain. Fasten off.

FRONT
Work 79 (85) ch sts for a base chain.

Row 1: 3 ch (to count as first dc of row), then 1 dc in each st of base chain.

Rows 2–4: Follow the directions on p. 95 to complete these 3 rows in vertical ribbing (= 1-¼ in [3 cm]).

Row 5: 3 ch (= first dc of row), then 1 dc in each st of base chain.

Rows 6–39 (43): Follow the chart on p. 117 and the instructions for honeycomb stitch, raised cables, and staggered clusters to form the pattern. In Rows 14 (16), 20 (22), 26 (28), and 30 (32) follow the instructions on p. 26-28 to inc by 1 st at each end of the row until, in Row 31 (33), you are working with 87 (93) sts. Cont straight in pattern to the end of Row 39 (43).

Armholes: Row 40 (44): Work forward with a sl st in each of the first 3 (4) sts, cont in pattern sts until 3 (4) sts remain; turn the work.

Next row: * Work forward with a sl st in each of the first 2 sts, cont in pattern sts until 2 sts remain; turn the work *. Rep from * to * once.

Next row: ** Work forward with a sl st in the first st, cont in pattern sts until 1 st remains; turn the work *. Rep from * to * twice = 67 (71) sts. Cont straight in pattern to the end of Row 63 (69).

Neck and shoulder: Next row: Pattern 34 (38), turn the work and pattern back to the armhole edge. Complete the 2 sides separately from this point, beg with left front.

Next row: With rs facing, pattern until 3 (4) sts remain (= neck edge); turn the work = 14 sts [end of Row 67 (71)].

Next row: With rs facing, work forward with a sl st over each of the first 8 sts, pattern to end; turn and work back toward armhole edge.

Next row: Work forward with a sl over each of the 6 remaining sts. Fasten off.

For the neck, count 33 sts across center front and rejoin the yarn with a sl st in the following st. Complete the right front as given for the left, reversing the shaping.

SLEEVE

Work 58 (64) ch sts for a base chain.

Row 1: 3 ch (to count as first dc) then work 1 dc in each st of base chain.

Rows 2–4: Follow the directions on p. 95 to complete these 3 rows in vertical ribbing (= 1-¼ in [3 cm]).

Row 5: 3 ch (= first dc) then work 1 dc in each st of base chain.

Rows 6–53 (57): Follow the chart to work the pattern in honeycomb st, raised cables, and staggered clusters.

Shoulder cap: Row 54 (58): Work forward with a sl st in each of the first 3 (4) sts, pattern until 3 (4) sts remain, turn the work and pattern to end.

Next row: * Work forward with a sl st in each of the next 2 sts, pattern until 2 sts remain; turn the work and pattern to end *. Rep from * to * 0 (1) time.

Next row: ** Work forward with a sl st in the first st, pattern until 1 st remains; turn the work and pattern to end **. Rep from ** to ** twice. ° Work 1 row straight. **(pattern continued on page 219)**

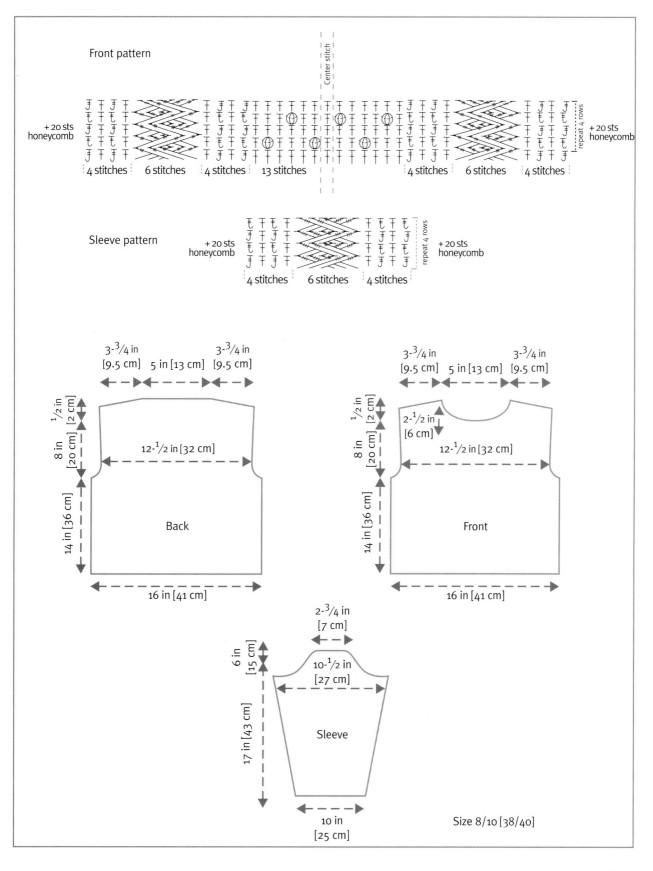

Front pattern

Center stitch

+ 20 sts honeycomb

4 stitches | 6 stitches | 4 stitches | 13 stitches | 4 stitches | 6 stitches | 4 stitches

repeat 4 rows

+ 20 sts honeycomb

Sleeve pattern

+ 20 sts honeycomb

4 stitches | 6 stitches | 4 stitches

repeat 4 rows

+ 20 sts honeycomb

3-3/4 in [9.5 cm]   5 in [13 cm]   3-3/4 in [9.5 cm]

1/2 in [2 cm]

8 in [20 cm]

12-1/2 in [32 cm]

14 in [36 cm]

Back

16 in [41 cm]

3-3/4 in [9.5 cm]   5 in [13 cm]   3-3/4 in [9.5 cm]

1/2 in [2 cm]

2-1/2 in [6 cm]

8 in [20 cm]

12-1/2 in [32 cm]

14 in [36 cm]

Front

16 in [41 cm]

2-3/4 in [7 cm]

6 in [15 cm]

10-1/2 in [27 cm]

17 in [43 cm]

Sleeve

10 in [25 cm]

Size 8/10 [38/40]

117

Japanese pillow

JAPANESE PILLOW

Materials

1 50g ball of Rowan "Felted Tweed" (50% merino wool, 25% alpaca, 25% viscose) each in

Bilberry no. 151, Rage no. 150, Phantom no. 153

1 4 mm crochet hook

1 darning or tapestry needle

1 pillow form measuring 9-$\frac{1}{2}$ X 15 in [24 X 38 cm]

Pins

Size

Finished pillow measures approximately

9-$\frac{1}{2}$ X 15 in [24 X 38 cm]

Stitches used

Double crochet (p. 49)

Honeycomb (p. 97)

Single crochet (p. 47)

Crab stitch (sc from left to right) (p. 45)

Mary quite contrary stitch (p. 106)

Skill level

* Beginner

TO MAKE

Beg with the red section, using Rage no. 150. Work 50 ch sts for a base chain.

Row 1: 3 ch (to count as first dc of row), then work 1 dc over each st of base chain.

Rows 2–24: Follow the directions on p. 106 to work every row in Mary quite contrary stitch. At completion of Row 24, fasten off.

Row 25: Join the brown (Phantom no. 153) yarn with a sl st, work 1 ch, then work 1 sc in each st of preceding row.

Rows 26–28: Work 1 sc in each st of preceding row. At completion of Row 28, fasten off.

Row 29: Join the violet (Bilberry no. 151) yarn with a sl st, work 3 ch, then follow the directions on p. 97 to work in honeycomb stitch.

Rows 30–43: Continue in honeycomb stitch.

Row 44: 3 ch, then work 1 dc in each st of previous row. Fasten off. Complete a second, identical section for the other half of the pillow.

OBI BELT

Using brown (Phantom no. 153), work 150 ch sts for a base chain.

Rows 1–4: 1 ch, then 1 sc over each st of previous row. At completion of Row 4, fasten off.

Join the red yarn with a sl st at one end of the belt and work 1 row of crab stitch (sc from left to right) on all 4 sides of the belt. Fasten off.

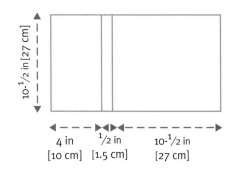

10-$\frac{1}{2}$ in [27 cm]

4 in [10 cm] $\frac{1}{2}$ in [1.5 cm]   10-$\frac{1}{2}$ in [27 cm]

ASSEMBLY

Place the 2 halves of the pillow rs tog and pin in place. Backstitch the seam on 3 sides, leaving one short side open. Turn the slip thus formed right side out, insert the pillow, and slipstitch the last seam. Tie the obi belt around the pillow over the brown stripe.

4
LACE PATTERNS

Lace patterns remain the standard for crochet technique. They have traditionally been used for making doilies, bedspreads, tablecloths, and other decorative and useful items for the home. Lace stitches are made up of motifs that are, in turn, made up of multiple chain stitches, resulting in a light and airy look. Worked with yarns other than the classic mercerized cotton—pile yarns, for example—lace patterns take on a more contemporary look that is right for wearables.

Simple Stitches

SHELLS

A shell is formed by working several stitches in a single stitch. To keep the work flat, it's necessary to skip one or more base stitches (as given in the pattern instructions) between the shells.

1. Skip the number of stitches indicated in the instructions.

2. Insert the hook in the next stitch.

3. Work 1 double crochet.

4. Continue working the number of dc indicated into the same stitch.

5. Skip the same number of stitches as before and work an identical shell in the following stitch.

PICOT FORMED OF 3 CHAIN STITCHES

1. Work 3 chain stitches.

2. Work 1 sc (or 1 sl st) in the 3rd of the sts just worked.

3. A picot can be made up of several chain stitches; the number is always indicated in the pattern stitch instructions.

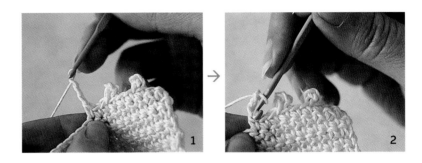

BUNDLES

1. Yarn over once.

2. Insert hook in stitch, yarn over.

3. Draw up a loop, slightly elongated.

4. Repeat these steps over as many stitches as indicated in the pattern stitch instructions.

5. To complete the bundle, yo and draw through all the loops on the hook at once, then work 1 ch st to keep the bundle in place.

Composite stitches

STAGGERED PICOTS

Work a multiple of 3 stitches plus 1 stitch for the base chain.

Row 1: 3 ch (to count as first double crochet), * in next st work 1 dc, 1 picot formed of 3 ch, and 1 dc, now work 1 ch, skip 2 sts *, repeat from * to * across the row. End by working 1 dc over the last st of the previous row.

Row 2: 3 ch (to count as first double crochet), * in next chain lp work 1 dc, 1 picot, and 1 dc, then work 2 ch *, repeat from * to * across the row. End by working 1 dc over the 3rd ch st at beg of previous row.

Following rows: Repeat Row 2.

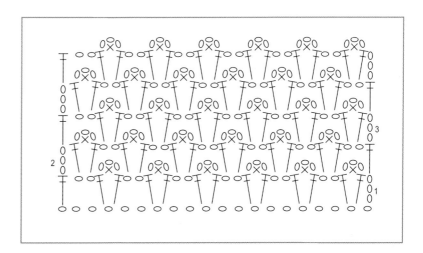

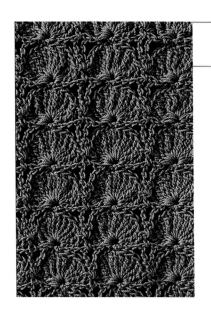

JAPANESE FANS

Work a multiple of 12 stitches plus 1 stitch for the base chain.

Row 1 (rs): 1 ch (to count as first sc), 1 sc in 2nd chain st from hook, * skip 5 sts, work 13 dbl tr in the foll ch st, skip 5 ch sts, work 1 sc in foll st *, repeat from * to * across the row. End by working 1 sc in the last ch st of the base chain.

Row 2: 5 ch (to count as first dbl tr), 1 dbl tr over first sc of previous row, * 4 ch, 1 sc in the 7th of 13 dbl tr in previous row, 4 ch, in next st work 1 dbl tr, 1 ch, 1 dbl tr *, rep from * to * across the row. End by working 2 dbl tr in last sc.

Row 3: 1 ch, 1 sc in first st, 13 dbl tr in foll sc, * 1 sc in ch lp bet next 2 dbl tr *, rep from * to * across the row. End by working 1 sc in the 5th ch st at beg of preceding row.

Following rows: Repeat Rows 2 and 3.

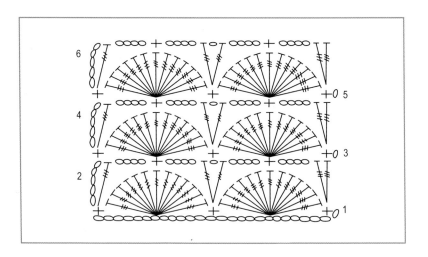

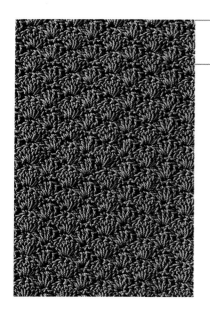

CLOSED GARLANDS

Work a multiple of 6 stitches plus 1 stitch for the base chain.

Row 1: 1 ch, 1 sc in 2nd ch st from hook, * skip 2 ch sts, 5 dc in following ch st, skip 2 ch sts, 1 sc in following ch st *, rep from * to *. End by working 1 sc in the last ch st of row.

Row 2: 3 ch (to count as first dc of row), 2 dc in first st, * skip 2 dc, work 1 sc in foll dc, skip 2 dc, work 5 dc in foll sc *, rep from * to * across the row. End by working 3 dc in the last sc of the row.

Row 3: 1 ch, 1 sc in first st, * skip 2 dc, work 5 dc in next sc, skip 2 dc, work 1 sc in foll dc *, rep from * to * across the row. End by working 1 sc in the 3rd ch st at beg of preceding row.

Following rows: Repeat Rows 2 and 3.

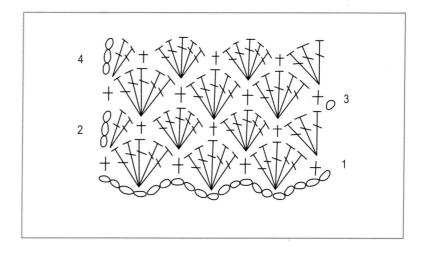

ARCADE STITCH

Work a multiple of 10 stitches plus 1 stitch for the base chain.

Row 1: 3 ch (to count as first dc of row), work 2 dc tog over 4th st from hook, * 2 ch, skip 2 sts, 5 dc, 2 ch, skip 2 sts, 5 dc tog *, rep from * to * across the row. End by working 3 dc tog over the last ch st of the row.

Row 2: 1 ch, 1 sc over next group of 3 dc tog, 2 sc, 1 sc over foll dc, * 5 ch, skip 3 dc, 7 sc *, rep from * to * across the row. End by working 4 sc.

Row 3: 1 ch, 1 sc over first st of row, * in next ch lp work 6 dc, 3 ch, and 6 dc, skip 3 sts, work 1 sc in the foll st *, rep from * to * across the row. End by working 1 sc over the last sc of the row.

Row 4: 9 ch, * 1 sc in next 3-st ch lp, 9 ch *, rep from * to * across the row. End by working 4 ch and 1 dbl tr over the last sc of the row.

Row 5: 3 ch (to count as first dc of row), 2 dc, * 2 ch, skip 2 sts, work 5 dc tog over foll sc, 2 ch, skip 2 sts, 5 dc *, rep from * to * across the row. End by working 3 dc.

Row 6: 6 ch, skip 2 sts, work * 7 sc, 5 ch, skip 3 sts *, rep from * to * across the row. End by working 2 ch sts, skip 1 st, and work 1 dc in 3rd ch st of preceding row.

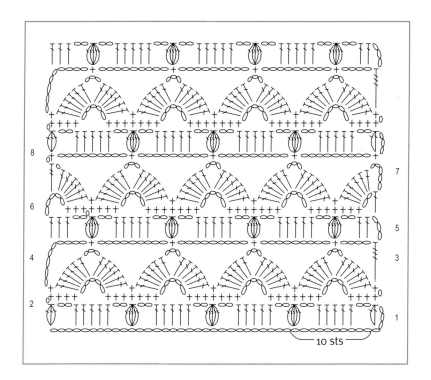

Row 7: 5 ch, in next 2-st ch lp work 6 dc, * skip 3 sts, work 1 sc over foll sc, skip 3 sts, then in next ch lp work 6 dc, 3 ch, 6 dc *, rep from * to * across the row. End by working 6 dc, 1 ch and 1 tr in final ch lp of row.

Row 8: 1 ch, 1 sc over tr in previous row, * 9 ch, 1 sc in next 3-st ch lp *, rep from * to * across the row. End by working 1 sc over the 4th ch st at beg of previous row.

Following rows: Repeat Rows 1–8.

SHELL STRIPES

Work a multiple of 8 stitches for the base chain.

Row 1: 3 ch (to count as first dc), 3 dc into 4th st from hook, skip 3 sts, * 1 sc over next st, skip 3 sts, work 7 dc (= 1 shell) into foll st, skip 3 sts *, rep from * to * across the row. End by working 1 shell formed of 4 dc into the last st of row.

Row 2: 5 ch * 1 half-dc in next sc, 3 ch, skip 3 sts, work 1 half-dc in foll dc, skip 3 sts *, rep from * to * across the row. End by working 1 half-dc over the 3rd ch st at beg of previous row.

Row 3: 5 ch, * 1 half-dc in next half-dc, 3 ch, skip 3 sts *, rep from * to * across the row. End by working 1 half-dc in 2nd ch st at beg of previous row.

Row 4: 1 ch, 1 sc over first half-dc, * 3 ch, 1 sc over foll half-dc *, rep from * to * across the row. End by working 1 sc over 2nd ch st at beg of previous row.

Row 5: 1 ch, 1 sc over first sc, * in next sc work 1 shell formed of 7 dc, 1 sc over foll sc *, rep from * to * across the row. End by working 1 sc in the last sc of the previous row.

Row 6: 5 ch, * 1 half-dc in 4th dc of foll shell, 3 ch, skip 3 sts, work 1 half-dc in foll sc, 3 ch *, rep from * to * across the row. End by working 1 half-dc over the last sc of the previous row.

Row 7: 5 ch, * 1 half-dc over next half-dc, 3 ch *, rep from * to * across the row. End by working 1 half-dc over the 2nd ch st at beg of previous row.

Row 8: 1 ch, 1 sc over first half-tr of row, * 3 ch, 1 sc over foll half-dc *, rep from * to * across the row. End by working 1 sc over the 2nd ch st at beg of previous row.

Following rows: Repeat Rows 1–8.

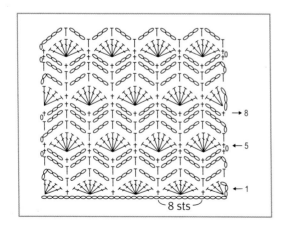

DAISY STITCH

Work a multiple of 10 stitches plus 1 stitch for the base chain.

Row 1: 1 ch (to count as first sc), 1 sc in foll st, 3 ch, and in same ch st as sc last worked, work 3 dc, * 2 ch, skip 4 sts, work 1 sc over next st, 2 ch, skip 4 sts, in foll st work [3 dc, 3 ch, 1 sc, 3 ch, 3 dc) *, rep from * to * across the row. End by working 3 dc, 3 ch, and 1 sc over the last st of the previous row.

Row 2: 6 ch, 1 sc in next ch lp, * 3 ch, 6 dc tog worked as (over next 3 dc, skip 2 ch lps, over next 3 dc), cont with 3 ch, 1 sc in next ch lp, 6 ch, 1 sc over foll ch lp *, rep from * to * across the row. End by working 1 sc in the last ch lp of the row, 2 ch, and 1 tr over the first sc of the previous row.

Row 3: 1 ch, 1 sc over tr, * 2 ch, in the top of the group of 6 dc tog work (3 dc, 3 ch, 1 sc, 3 ch, 3 dc), cont with 2 ch, 1 sc in the next 5-st ch lp *, rep from * to * across the row. End by working 1 sc over the 4th ch st at beg of previous row.

Row 4: 4 ch, over next 3 dc of previous row work 3 dc tog, 3 ch, * 1 sc in next ch lp, 5 ch, 1 sc in foll ch lp, 3 ch, 6 dc tog worked as (over the next 3 dc, skip 2 ch lps, over the foll 3 dc), 3 ch *, rep from * to * across the row. End by working tog 3 dc plus 1 tr over the last 4 sts of the previous row.

Following rows: Repeat Rows 1–4.

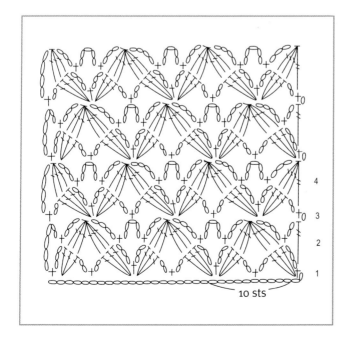

10 sts

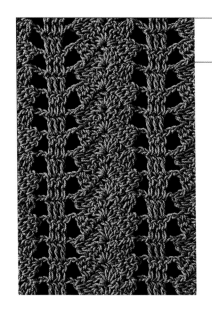

EARS OF WHEAT

Work a multiple of 16 stitches for the base chain.

Row 1: 3 ch (to count as first dc), work 1 dc over 5th ch st from hook, 1 dc in next st, * 2 ch sts, skip 6 ch sts, over foll st work (3 dc, 2 ch, 1 dc, 2 ch, 3 dc), 2 ch, skip 6 ch sts, 3 dc *, rep from * to * across the row. End by working 3 dc.

Row 2: 3 ch (= dc), 2 dc, * 2 ch, 3 dc tog over next 3 dc of previous row, 1 ch, skip next ch lp, over foll dc work (3 dc, 1 ch, 1 dc, 1 ch, 3 dc), cont with 1 ch, 3 dc tog over foll 3 dc of previous row, 2 ch, skip next 2-st ch lp, work 3 dc over foll 3 dc of previous row *, rep from * to * across the row. End by working 2 dc then 1 dc over the 3rd ch st at beg of previous row.

Row 3: 3 ch (= 1 dc), skip the first st, work 2 dc, * 2 ch, skip next 2 ch lps, work 3 dc tog over the next 3 dc of the previous row, 1 ch, skip next ch lp, over foll dc work (3 dc, 1 ch, 1 dc, 1 ch, 3 dc), 1 ch, work 3 dc tog over the next 3 dc of the previous row, 2 ch, skip foll 2-st ch lp, work 3 dc over the next 3 dc of the previous row *, rep from * to * across the row. End by working 2 dc then 1 dc over the 3rd ch st at beg of previous row.

Following rows: Repeat Row 3.

16 sts

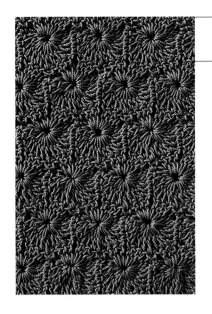

HEXAGONS

Work a multiple of 8 chain stitches plus 4 stitches for a base chain.

Row 1 (ws): 1 ch, 1 sc over 2nd st from hook, 1 sc in each of next 3 ch sts (= 1 bar), skip 3 ch sts, work 3 dc over foll ch st, skip 3 ch sts, work 1 sc over foll ch st, * skip 3 sts, over foll ch st work (3 dc, 1 bar, 3 dc), skip 3 ch sts, work 1 sc over foll ch st *, rep from * to * across the row. End by working 1 sc over the last ch st of the row.

Row 2: 4 ch (to count as first tr of row), over the next 8 sts work (yo, insert hook, yo and draw up a lp, slightly extend this last lp) , then yo, work all the loops off the hook at once (= bundle), then work 1 ch st to hold the bundle firmly, 4 ch, 1 sc at top of bar in previous row, * 4 ch, 1 bundle over the next 15 sts (follow chart and work over the 4 ch sts on the other side of the bar, the next 3 dc, the sc, the foll 3 dc, then the 4 sc of the following bar), 4 ch, 1 dc at top of next bar *, rep from * to * across the row. End by working 1 complete bundle.

Row 3: 1 ch, 1 sc over first st, * over st closing the next bundle work (3 dc, 1 bar, 3 dc), 1 dc over foll sc *, rep from * to * across the row. End by working 4 dc over the stitch closing the last bundle of the previous row.

Row 4: 8 ch (to count as 1 tr and 3 ch), beg in 5th st from hook work 1 bundle over the next 15 sts, * 3 ch, 1 sc at top of bar, 3 ch, 1 bundle over the foll 15 sts *, rep from * to * across the row. End by working 1 bundle over the last 8 sts of the previous row.

Row 5: 9 ch, work 1 sc in 2nd ch st from hook, 1 sc in each of the next 3 ch sts (= 1 dc plus 1 bar), 3 dc in first sc, 1 sc over foll sc, * over st closing next bundle work (3 dc, 1 bar, 3 dc), cont with 1 sc over foll sc *, rep from * to * across the row. End by working 1 sc in the 4th ch st at beg of previous row.

HARLEQUIN STITCH

Work a multiple of 10 chain stitches plus 6 stitches for a base chain.

Row 1 (ws): 1 ch, 1 sc in 2nd st from hook, 1 sc over next st, * skip 3 ch sts, work 7 dc in foll ch st, skip 3 ch sts, work 3 sc over next 3 sts *, rep from * to * across the row. End by working 4 dc over the last ch st of row.

Row 2: 1 ch, 1 sc in each of the next 2 sts, * 3 ch, over the next 7 sts work (yo, insert hook, yo and draw up a lp, slightly extend this last lp) , then yo, work all the loops off the hook at once (= bundle), then work 1 ch st to hold the bundle firmly (see chart), 3 ch, 1 sc over each of the next 3 sts *, rep from * to * across the row. end by working 3 ch, 1 bundle over the last 4 sts of the row.

Row 3: 3 ch (= 1 dc), 3 dc over first st, * 1 sc in each of the next 3 sc, 7 dc into st closing following bundle *, rep from * to * across the row. End by working 1 sc in each of the last 2 sc of the previous row.

Row 4: 3 ch (= 1 dc), skip the first st, over the foll 3 sts work 1 bundle, then * 3 ch, 1 sc in each of the next 3 sts, 3 ch, over the foll 7 sts work 1 bundle *, rep from * to * across the row. End by working 3 ch, 1 sc over foll st, 1 sc in the 3rd of the 3 ch sts at beg of previous row.

Row 5: 1 ch, 1 sc in each of the first 2 sc of previous row, * 7 dc into st closing next bundle, 1 sc in each of the foll 3 sc *, rep from * to * across the row. end by working 4 dc over the 3rd of 3 ch sts at beg of previous row.

Following rows: Repeat Rows 2–5.

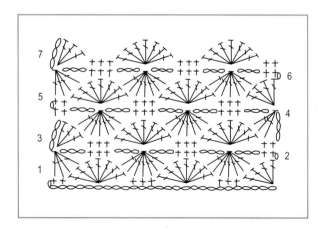

GARLAND STRIPES

Work a multiple of 10 chain stitches plus 1 stitch for a base chain.

Row 1 (ws): Work 1 sc in the 2nd st from hook, * 3 ch, cross 2 dc as follows: (skip 5 sts, work 1 dc in foll ch st, 5 ch, pass hook behind first dc and work 1 dc in 4th of the 5 ch last worked), 3 ch, skip 3 sts, 1 sc *, rep from * to * across the row. End by working 1 sc over the last ch st of the row.

Row 2: 3 ch (= 1 dc), skip the first st of the 3-st ch lp, work * 11 dc into foll 5-st ch lp, 1 puff st formed of 3 half-dc in next sc, 1 ch *, rep from * to * across the row. End by working 1 dc in the last sc of the row.

Row 3: 2 ch, skip 2 dc, work 1 half-dc in foll dc, 4 ch, 1 half-tr in top of preceding half-tr, cont with * 3 ch, skip 3 dc, work 1 sc over foll dc, 3 ch, cross 2 dc as follows: (1 dc in 2nd of group of 11 dc, 5 ch, pass hook behind previous dc and work 1 dc in 10th of preceding group of 11 dc) *, rep from * to * across the row. End by working the first of 2 crossed dc at the top of the chain, working only 2 (instead of 5) ch sts bet the 2 crossed dc.

Row 4: 3 ch (= 1 dc), 5 dc into 2-st ch lp, * 1 puff st formed of 3 half-dc in next sc, 1 ch, 11 dc into foll 5-st ch lp *, rep from * to * across the row. End by working 6 dc in the last ch lp of the previous row.

Row 5: 1 ch, 1 sc in first st, 3 ch, 2 crossed dc as follows: (1 dc in 2nd of foll group of 11 dc, 5 ch, pass hook behind previous dc and work 1 dc in 5th of preceding group of 6 dc), * 3 ch, skip 3 dc, work 1 sc over foll dc, 3 ch, 1 dc in 2nd of foll group of dc, 5 ch, pass hook behind dc just worked and work 1 dc in 10th dc of same group as before *, rep from * to * across the row. End by working 3 ch, 1 sc at top of chain.

Following rows: Repeat Rows 1–5.

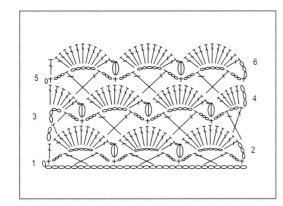

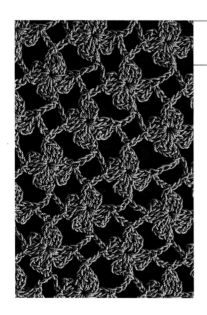

DAISY CHAIN STITCH

The base chain forms in the course of Row 1.

Row 1 (rs): 7 ch, * 1 sl st in 4th st from hook, 3 ch, into ring just formed work (2 dc, 3 ch, 1 sl st, 3 ch 2 dc), 10 ch *, rep from * to * until you have formed the required number of daisies across the width of your work. End the row by omitting the 10 ch sts that conclude each pattern repeat.

Note: Do not turn the work; continue Row 2 along the other side of Row 1. Be careful not to twist Row 1 as you work the following row.

Row 2 (rs): * 3 ch, 1 sl st in central ring of following daisy, 3 ch, into the same ring work (2 dc, 3 ch, 1 sl st [= 1 complete central petal], then 3 ch, 2 dc), skip 2 ch sts of base chain linking 2 daisies, 1 sl st in foll ch st, 7 ch, skip 2 ch sts, work 1 sl st in foll st *, rep from * to * across the row.

Row 3 (ws): 11 ch, 1 sl st in 4th st from hook, 3 ch, 2 dc into ring previously formed, 3 ch, 1 sl st at top of 3 ch sts in central petal of preceding daisy in preceding row (see chart). Now work * 10 ch, 1 sl st in 4th st from hook, 3 ch, 2 dc in ring previously formed, 1 sl st in the 4th of 7 ch sts in the next ch lp, 3 ch, and into the same ring as the 2 previous dc work (1 sl st, 3 ch, 2 dc, 3 ch, 1 sl st) at top of 3 ch sts of central petal of following daisy *, rep from * to * across the row.

Row 4 (rs): 9 ch, skip 2 ch sts, work 1 sl st in next ch st, * 3 ch, 1 sl st into ring of daisy, 3 ch, into same ring work (2 dc, 3 ch, 1 sl st, 3 ch, 2 dc), skip 2 ch sts, work 1 sl st in foll ch st, 7 ch, skip the next 6 sts, work 1 sl st over foll ch st *, rep from * to * across the row. End by working 3 ch, 1 sl st into ring of last daisy, 3 ch, 2 dc into same ring as before.

Row 5 (ws): * 10 ch, 1 sl st in 4th st from hook, 3 ch, 2 dc into ring previously formed, 1 sl st into 4th ch st of foll ch lp, 3 ch, into same ring as the previous 2 dc work (1 sl st, 3 ch, 2 dc), 1 sl st at top of the 3 ch sts of the central petal of the next daisy *, rep from * to * across the row. End the daisy by omitting the last 3 ch sts and 1 sl st.

Following rows: Repeat Rows 2–5.

As given, daisy chain stitch has a half-daisy along the left edge. To make a pretty border and complete the flowers, rejoin the yarn with a sl st where indicated by a arrow on the chart then work as follows: * 3 ch, into ring of daisy work (1 sl st, 3 ch, 2 dc, 3 ch, 1 sl st, 3 ch, 2 dc), skip 3 ch sts, work 1 sl st into foll ch st, 6 ch, 1 sl st into last ch st before central petal of next daisy *, rep from * to * along the edge. End the border by omitting the last 6 ch sts and the sl st at the edge of the final daisy.

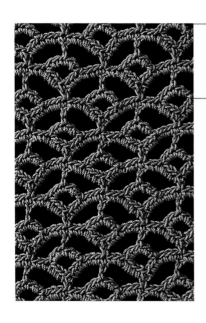

STAGGERED DOUBLE LOOPS

Work a multiple of 10 chain stitches plus 1 stitch for a base chain.

Row 1 (ws): 8 ch, work 1 sc over 14th st from hook, * 5 ch, skip 4 ch sts, 1 dc over next st, 5 ch, skip 4 ch sts, 1 sc over foll st *, rep from * to * across the row. End by working 5 ch, skip 4 ch sts, work 1 dc over last ch st.

Row 2: 1 ch, 1 sc over dc, * 6 sc into foll ch lp, 1 sc over foll sc, 3 sc in next ch lp, (4 ch, then without turning the work, go back and work 1 sl st in the 4th of 6 sc in the previous lp, then again working from right to left work 5 sc in 4-st ch lp just formed = 1 double-back loop), 3 sc in same ch lp as preceding 3 sc, 1 sc over foll dc *, rep from * to * across the row. End by working 3 sc after forming the final double back loop, wok 1 sc in 4th ch st at beg of previous row.

Row 3: 1 ch, 1 sc in first st, * 5 ch, 1 dc in central st of foll double back loop, 5 ch, 1 sc in 4th foll sc (i.e., skip 3 sc and work into sc over the dc 2 rows below; see chart) *. Rep from * to * across the row. End by working 1 sc in the last sc of the row.

Row 4: 1 ch, 1 sc over sc, 3 sc in foll ch lp, turn the work, continue with 2 ch, 1 dc over first sc of row, 1 ch, turn the work again with rs facing, work 1 sc in dc just formed, 2 dc in 2-st ch lp, 3 sc in same lp as previous 3 sc, * 1 sc in next dc, 6 sc in foll 5-st ch lp, 1 sc over foll sc, 3 sc in next ch lp, 1 double back loop, 3 sc in same ch lp as preceding 3 sc *, rep from * to * across the row. End by working 5 ch, 1 double back loop, but work only 3 sc (instead of 5) in this lp.

Row 5: 8 ch, * 1 sc in foll sc above dc 2 rows below, 5 ch, 1 dc in 3rd central sc of foll double back loop, 5 ch *, rep from * to * across row. End by working 1 dc over the last sc of the previous row.

Following rows: Repeat Rows 2–5.

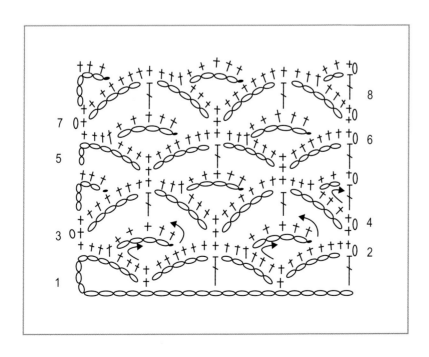

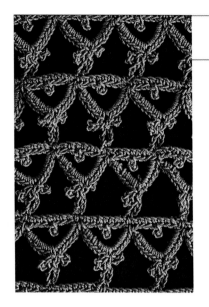

CROWNED LOOPS

Work a multiple of 8 chain stitches for a base chain.

Row 1: 1 ch, skip 1 st of the base chain, (4 sc, 1 picot formed of 3 ch over last sc worked, 4 sc, 9 ch then, without turning the work, work back over the sts just formed with 1 sl st in the 8th sc to the right, and again work from right to left with 7 sc in the loop just formed (5 ch, 1 sl st in the 5th ch st from hook, 7 ch, 1 sl st in 7th ch st from hook, 5 ch, 1 sl st in 5th ch st from hook = 1 crown), 7 sc in same loop as previously formed *. Rep from * to * across the row. End by working 1 sl st over the last ch st of the row.

Row 2: 11 ch sts (counts as 1 triple treble plus 4 ch sts), * 1 sc in central 7-st ch lp of next crown, 7 ch *; rep from * to * across the row. End by working 1 tr tr in last sc of row.

Row 3: 1 ch, 1 sc over tr tr, 1 sc in each of the next 2 ch sts, 1 sc over foll sc, turn the work and continue with 4 ch, 1 tr over first sc of row, again turn the work, 8 ch, 1 sl st in the 7th ch st from hook, 5 ch, 1 sl st in 5th ch s from hook (= $\frac{1}{2}$ crown), 7 sc into 4-st ch lp, * 1 sc over each of the next 4 ch sts, 1 picot formed of 3 ch sts, 1 sc in each of the foll 4 ch sts, 9 ch sts, 1 sl st in the 8th sc to the right, 7 sc in loop thus formed, 1 crown, 7 sc in same lp *. Rep from * to * across the row. End by working 1 sc in each of the 4 sts of the chain, 9 ch, 1 sl st over 4th sc to the right, 7 sc in loop thus formed, 5 ch, 1 sl st in 5th ch st from hook (= $\frac{1}{2}$ crown), 1 sc in same loop. 3 ch, 1 tr in last sc of row.

Row 4: 1 ch, 1 sc over foll ch st, * 7 ch, 1 sc in central ch lp of foll crown *, rep from * to * across the row, End by working 1 sc over the last 8-st ch lp.

Row 5: 1 ch, 1 sc over first st, 1 sc in each of next 3 ch sts, * 1 picot formed of 3 ch, 1 sc in each of the next 3 ch sts, 1 sc over foll sc, 9 ch sts, 1 sl st in the 8th sc to the right, now work 7 sc, 1 crown, and 7 sc in the loop thus formed, 1 sc in each of the next 4 ch sts *. Rep from * to * across the row. End by working 1 sl st over the last sc of the row.

Following rows: Repeat Rows 2–5.

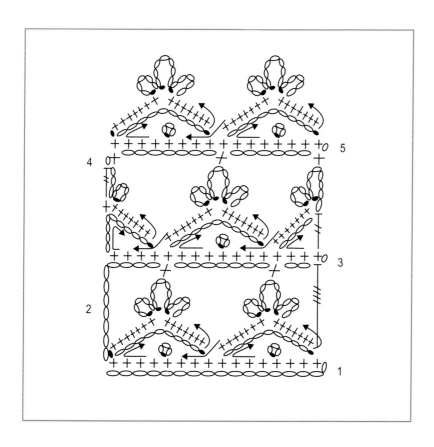

LACE FANS

Work a multiple of 12 chain stitches plus 1 chain stitch for a base chain.

Row 1: 1 ch, 1 sc in 2nd st from hook, * 5 ch, skip 3 ch sts, 1 sc in next ch st *, rep from * to * across the row. End by working 1 sc in last st of base chain.

Row 2: 5 ch (to count as 1 dc plus 2 ch sts, * 1 sc in next ch lp, 8 dc in foll ch lp, 1 sc in next ch lp, 5 ch *, rep from * to * across the row. End by working 2 ch, 1 dc over last sc of row.

Row 3: 1 ch, 1 sc over dc, * work (1 dc over foll dc, 3 ch, 1 sl st in top of last dc to form a picot) 7 times, 1 dc over foll dc, 1 sc in next ch lp *. Rep from * to * across the row. End by working 1 sc in the 3rd ch st at beg of previous row.

Row 4: 8 ch, skip 2 picots, * 1 sc over next picot, 5 ch, skip 1 picot, 1 sc over foll picot, 5 ch, 1 dc in next sc bet 2 fans, 5 ch, skip 2 picots *, rep from * to * across the row. End by working 5 ch and 1 dc over last sc of row.

Following rows: Repeat Rows 2–4.

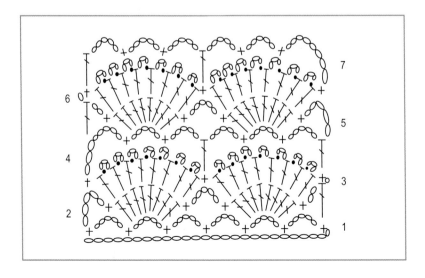

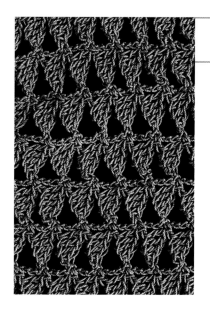

EYELET PYRAMIDS

Work a multiple of 4 chain stitches plus 1 chain stitch for a base chain.

Row 1: 1 ch, 1 sc in 2nd st from hook, * work (6 ch, 1 sc in 3rd st from hook, 1 dc in each of the foll 3 ch sts = 1 pyramid), skip 3 ch sts, 1 sc in next ch st of base chain *, rep from * to * across the row. End by working 1 sc in the last ch st of the row.

Row 2: 6 ch (to count as 1 dbl tr plus 1 ch st), work * 1 sc in ch st at tip of next pyramid, 3 ch *, rep from * to * across the row. End by working 1 ch, 1 dbl tr over last sc of row.

Row 3: 10 ch sts, 1 sc over foll sc, * 1 pyramid, 1 sc in foll sc *, rep from * to * across the row. End by working 5 ch, skip 1 ch st, work 1 dbl tr in next ch st.

Row 4: 1 ch, 1 sc in first st, * 3 ch, 1 sc in ch st at tip of next pyramid *, rep from * to * across the row. End by working 1 sc at center of 10-st ch lp.

Row 5: 1 ch, 1 sc over first st, * 1 pyramid, 1 sc over foll sc *, rep from * to * across the row. End by working 1 sc over last sc of row.

Following rows: Repeat Rows 2–5.

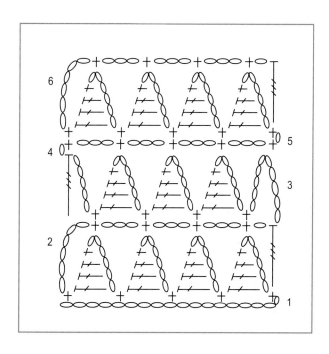

Shade trim

SHADE TRIM

Materials

1 50g ball of Coats "Aida" yarn (100% cotton)

Ficelle no. 390

1 1.75 mm crochet hook

A length of sheer linen fabric measuring 24 X 60 in [60 X 150 cm]

String-colored sewing thread

1 crewel needle

Pins

Sizes

Finished shade border as given measures 21-1/2 in wide X 5-3/4 in deep [55 X 14.5 cm]

Stitches used

Crowned loops (p.140)

Double crochet (p. 49)

Skill level

** Some experience

TO MAKE

You can adapt this border to any width according to the size of your window. Change the size by increasing or decreasing the number of multiples of 8 stitches (= 1 complete motif) in the base chain.

Rows 1–3: 3 ch, then work 1 dc in each st of the preceding row.

Rows 4–16: Follow the directions on p. 140 to complete 3 rows of crowed loops. At the completion of Row 16, fasten off.

ASSEMBLY

1. Press $1/4$ in then another $5/8$ in to the wrong side along each long edge of the linen. Stitch the hem thus formed $1/2$ in from the edge.

2. Along the lower edge of the linen, press under $1/4$ in then another $3/4$ in. Stitch $5/8$ in from the edge.

3. Make a casing at the top edge of the linen to fit the type of curtain rod or shade roller you have chosen.

4. Darn in all the yarn ends of the border.

5. Pin the border out to size, wrong side up, on a thick towel and press it under a damp cloth.

6. Place the edge of the border (the first 3 rows in double crochet) over the hem at the lower edge of the shade, pin, then tack in position. Using the needle and string-colored thread, slipstitch the border to the fabric.

Crib blanket

CRIB BLANKET

Materials

6 25g balls of Gedifra "Easy Soft" yarn (48% mohair, 42% polyamide, 10% cashmere)

Beige no. 8604

1 4 mm and 1 3.5 mm crochet hook

1 darning or tapestry needle

Pins

Sizes

Finished shade border as given measures 27-^{1}/$_2$ in [70 cm] square.

Stitches used

Half-double crochet (p.41)

Slip stitch (p. 40)

Daisy stitch (p. 131)

Skill level

** Some experience

TO MAKE

Using the 4 mm crochet hook, work 111 ch sts for a base chain (= 24-^{1}/$_2$ in [62 cm]).

Work in daisy stitch to form a square 24-^{1}/$_2$ in [62 cm] on a side. At the completion of the final row, fasten off.

Border: Using the 3.5 mm hook, rejoin the yarn with a sl st at a corner and work 100 sl sts evenly along each side of the square.

Rnd 1: 2 ch, then work * 1 treble over each sl st as far as the corner. Into corner st work 2 tr, 2 ch, 2 tr *, and rep from * to * along the other 3 sides. Close the round by working 1 sl st over the 2nd ch st at beg.

Rnds 2–8: Rep Row 1. At the completion of Rnd 8, fasten off.

FINISHING

Using the darning or tapestry needle, darn in the yarn ends.

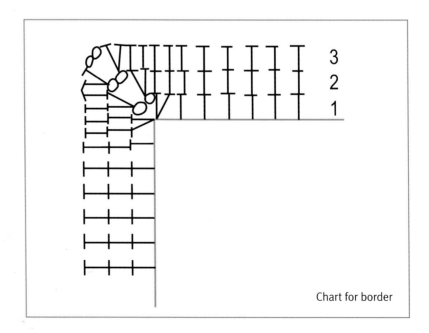

Chart for border

Lacy scarf

LACY SCARF

Materials

3 25g balls of Gedifra "Easy Soft" yarn (48% mohair, 42% polyamide, 10% cashmere)

Rose Pivoine no. 8646

1 4 mm crochet hook

1 darning or tapestry needle

A 5-in [12-cm] square of strong cardboard

Scissors

Size

Finished scarf measures 10 X 43 in [25 X 110 cm].

Stitches used

Arcade stitch (p.128)

Double crochet (p. 49)

Skill level

* Beginner

TO MAKE

Work 51 ch sts for a base chain (= 5 arcade motifs).
Follow the directions on p. 128 to work arcade stitch for a length of approximately 43 in [110 cm], completing 21 rows of motifs.
Next row: Work 3 ch (to count as first dc of row), then work 1 dc over each st of the preceding row.

FINISHING

Using the darning or tapestry needle, darn in all the yarn ends.
Fringe: Wind the yarn 200 times around the cardboard, as shown in the chart. Cut through all strands of yarn at one edge of the cardboard. Divide the strands into hanks of 10 strands each. Fold each hank in half and use the hook to knot 10 hanks through the first and last rows of the scarf. Trim the ends of the fringe even.

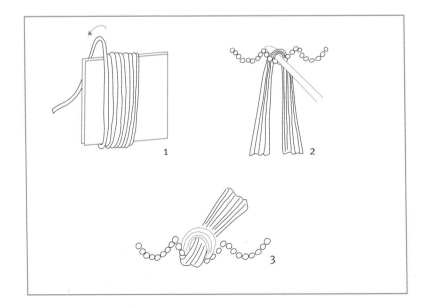

Slippers

SLIPPERS

Materials

2 50g balls of Coats "Cotton Wool" yarn (50% wool, 50% cotton)

Dream no. 929

1 3.5 mm crochet hook

1 darning or tapestry needle

1 crewel needle

About 20 in [50 cm] of $3/4$-in wide grosgrain ribbon

Beige sewing thread

Safety pin

Sizes

Size 1 = 10 in [25 cm]

Size 2 = 11-$1/2$ in [29 cm] long

Stitches used

Harlequin stitch (p.134)

Single crochet (p. 47)

Crab stitch (sc from left to right) (p.45)

Skill level:

** Some experience

TO MAKE

UPPER (SIZES 1 AND 2)

Work the upper in rounds. Work 4 ch sts for a base chain and join the last st to the first with a sl st to form a ring.

Rnd 1: 1 ch, then into central ring work 6 sc. Close with a sl st over the first ch st of rnd.

Rnd 2: 1 ch, then attach the safety pin or a contrasting yarn marker to indicate the beg of this and the following rnds. Move the safety pin up a row or two as the work grows. Work 2 sc over each st of preceding rnd and close with a sl st over the ch st at beg of rnd = 12 sts.

Rnd 3: 1 ch, 1 sc in each st of preceding rnd. Close by working 1 sl st in the ch st at beg of rnd.

Rnd 4: 1 ch, then work * 2 sc in next st, 1 sc in foll st *. Rep from * to * to end of rnd. Close with a sl st over the ch st at beg of rnd = 18 sts.

Rnd 5: 1 ch, 1 sc in each st of preceding rnd. Close by working 1 sl st in the ch st at beg of rnd.

Rnd 6: 1 ch, 1 sc over first st of preceding rnd, then work 1 sc in each of the next 4 sts, * 2 sc in foll st, 1 sc in each of the next 5 sts *. Rep from * to * to end of rnd. Close by working 1 sl st in ch st at beg of rnd = 21 sts.

Rnd 7: 1 ch, 1 sc in each st of preceding rnd. Close by working 1 sl st in the ch st at beg of rnd.

Rnd 8: 1 ch, 1 sc in first st, work 1 sc in each of next 5 sts, * 2 sc in next st, 1 sc in each of next 6 sts *. Rep from * to * to end of rnd. Close by working 1 sl st over the ch st at beg of rnd = 24 sts.

Rnd 9: 1 ch, 1 sc in each st of preceding rnd. Close by working 1 sl st in the ch st at beg of rnd.

Rnd 10: 1 ch, 1 sc in first st, work 1 sc in each of next 6 sts, * 2 sc in next st, 1 sc in each of next 7 sts *. Rep from * to * to end of rnd. Close by working 1 sl st over the ch st at beg of rnd = 27 sts.

Rnd 11: 1 ch, 1 sc in each st of preceding rnd. Close by working 1 sl st in the ch st at beg of rnd.

Rnd 12: 1 ch, 1 sc in first st, work 1 sc in each of next 7 sts, * 2 sc in next st, 1 sc in each of next 8 sts *. Rep from * to * to end of rnd. Close by working 1 sl st over the ch st at beg of rnd = 30 sts.

Rnd 13: 1 ch, 1 sc in each st of preceding rnd. Close by working 1 sl st in the ch st at beg of rnd.

Rnd 14: 1 ch, 1 sc in first st, work 1 sc in each of next 8 sts, * 2 sc in next st, 1 sc in each of next 9 sts *. Rep from * to * to end of rnd. Close by working 1 sl st over the ch st at beg of rnd = 33 sts.

Now proceed according to size as follows.

SIZE 2:

Rnd 15: 1 ch, 1 sc in each st of preceding rnd. Close by working 1 sl st in the ch st at beg of rnd.

Rnd 16: 1 ch, 1 sc in first st, work 1 sc in each of next 9 sts, * 2 sc in next st, 1 sc in each of next 10 sts *. Rep from * to * to end of rnd. Close by working 1 sl st over the ch st at beg of rnd = 37 sts.

Rnd 17: 1 ch, 1 sc in each st of preceding rnd. Close by working 1 sl st in the ch st at beg of rnd.

Rnd 18: 1 ch, 1 sc in first st, work 1 sc in each of next 10 sts, * 2 sc in next st, 1 sc in each of next 11 sts *. Rep from * to * to end of rnd. Close by working 1 sl st over the ch st at beg of rnd = 42 sts.

BOTH SIZES:

Next rnd: 1 ch, 1 sc in each st of preceding rnd. Close by working 1 sl st in the ch st at beg of rnd. Repeat this round until upper measures 5-1/2 (6-1/4) in [14 (16) cm] from initial ring. Remove the safety pin.

SOLE (SIZES 1 AND 2)

Work the sole and the sides in rows of harlequin stitch.

Row 1: Turn the work, 1 ch, and follow the directions on p. 134 to work harlequin pattern stitch over 25 sts.

Row 2: Repeat Row 1.

Row 3: 3 ch (to count as first dc of row), 4 dc (instead of 3) in first st of row, then cont in harlequin pattern st.

Row 4: 3 ch, then work the first half-bundle as follows: work 1 dc over first st, work 2 dc over 2nd st of row, and work 1 dc over 3rd dc of row, then continue harlequin pattern stitch as given in the instructions.

Row 5: Work in harlequin stitch.

Row 6: Work in harlequin stitch and end the row by working 1 bundle formed of 7 dc, 3 ch, and 1 sc over each of the 3 sts of the preceding pattern row.

Row 7: Work in harlequin stitch and end by working 4 dc (instead of 3) in last st.

Row 8: Beg by working 3 sc (instead of 2), continue in harlequin stitch and end with a half-bundle formed of 4 dc (instead of 3).

Row 9: 3 ch, work 6 dc (instead of 3) into first sc, then continue in harlequin stitch. End by working 4 sc (instead of 2).

Rows 10–13: Continue working in harlequin stitch, increasing as established at beg and end of rows. On completing Row 13, continue according to size as follows.

Size 1: At completion of Row 13, fasten off.

Size 2: Rows 14–15: Work in harlequin stitch, increasing as before. At completion of Row 15, fasten off.

Make a second, identical slipper.

ASSEMBLY

Darn in all the yarn ends. Place the 2 sides of the heel ws tog and, with rs facing, work a row of single crochet for 2-1/4 in, starting at the top. Now turn the heel inside out, hold the sides at right angles to the crochet seam, and use the darning or tapestry needle to work a row of backstitch, forming a "T" seam at the bottom of the heel (see chart).

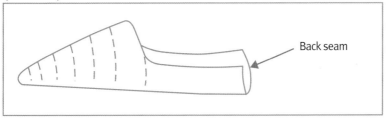

Back seam

FINISHING

Border: Rejoin the yarn with a sl st at the back seam. Work 1 ch, then work 1 rnd of single crochets (st over st) around the edge of the slipper. Close with a sl st over the ch st at beg. Now work 1 ch, and cont with a row of sc from left to right. Close with a sl st over the ch st at beg and fasten off.

Cut 2 pieces of grosgrain ribbon each 5 in [13 cm] long. Form 2 flat bows 2-1/4 in [5.5 cm] wide by folding the ends to the middle and placing a strip at the center (see photo). Slipstitch a bow to the upper of each slipper. Cut the remaining grosgrain ribbon in half and fold each length in half to make a loop. Sew a loop to the inside heel of each slipper, allowing 1 in [2.5 cm] to show above the heel.

Tank top

TANK TOP

Materials

6 25g balls of Rowan
"Kidsilk Night" yarn
(67% kid mohair, 18% silk,
10% polyester, 5% Nylon)

Macbeth no. 614

1 3 mm crochet hook

1 darning or tapestry needle

Pins

Sizes

US 8/10 (12/14) [EUR 38/40
(42/44)

Instructions for the
larger size are shown in
parentheses. When only
one number is given,
it applies to both sizes.

Stitches used

Double crochets (p.42)

Japanese fans (p. 126)

Skill level

** Some experience

TO MAKE

BACK

°Work 80 (88) ch sts for a base chain.

Rows 1–4: 3 ch, then 1 dc over each st of preceding row.

Row 5: Repeat Row 1, and follow the directions on p. 26–28 to inc by 1 st at each end of the row.

Rows 6–9: Repeat Row 1.

Row 10: Repeat Row 5.

Rows 11–14: Repeat Row 1.

Row 15: Repeat Row 5.

Rows 16–19: Repeat Row 1.

Row 20: Repeat Row 5.

Rows 21–24: Repeat Row 1.

Row 25: Repeat Row 5 = 90 (98) sts.

Cont straight in dc (as for Row 1) to the end of Row 30 (34).

Armholes: Next row: Work forward with a sl st over each of the first 3 (4) sts, pattern until 3 (4) sts remain, turn and work back to beg of row.

Next row: * Work forward with a sl st over each of the first 2 sts, pattern until 2 sts remain, turn and work back to beg of row *. Rep from * to *.

Next row: ** Work forward with a sl st over the first st, pattern until 1 st remains, turn and work back to beg of row **. Rep from ** to ** 1 (2) times = 72 (76) sts °.

Cont straight in dc to the end of Row 54 (58).

Neck and Shoulders: Next row: Work forward with a sl st over each of the first 8 (9) sts, pattern 12 (13), turn. Complete the 2 sides separately from this point, beg with right back.

Next row: Work forward with a sl st over each of the first 3 sts (= neck edge), pattern to end.

Next row: Pattern 9 (10) and fasten off.

Count 32 sts across the center back for the neck and join the yarn with a sl st in the following st. Complete the left back to match the right, reversing the shaping.

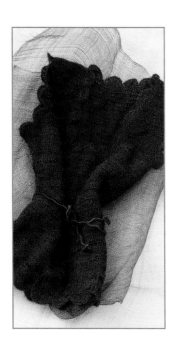

FRONT

As for back from ° to ° .

Cont straight in dc to the end of Row 34 (38).

Neck and Shoulders: Next row: Pattern 29 (30) and turn. Complete the 2 sides separately from this point, beg with left front.

Next row: Work forward with a sl st in each of the next 3 sts (= neck edge), pattern to end.

Next row: * Pattern until 2 sts remain, turn and work back to beg of row *. Rep from * to * once.

Work 2 rows straight.

Next row: Pattern until 1 st remains, turn and pattern back to beg of row. Rep this 1-st neck dec every 3 rows 4 times and, at the same time, after completing Row 54 (58) shape the shoulders as follows:

Row 55 (59): Beg at armhole edge, work forward with a sl st over each of the next 8 (9) sts, pattern to end, turn and work back to beg of row.

Next row: Work forward with a sl st over each of the next 9 (10) sts. Fasten off.

Count 14 sts across center front for the neck and rejoin the yarn with a sl st in the following st. Complete the right front to match the left, reversing the shaping.

ASSEMBLY

Darn in all the yarn ends. Place back and front rs tog and backstitch the shoulder and side seams.

BORDERS AND NECK

Rejoin the yarn with a sl st at left shoulder seam. Following the instructions on p. 126 for Japanese fan stitch, work 4 fan motifs down the left front, 3 motifs across the front neck, 4 motifs up the right front, and 4 motifs across the back neck = 15 motifs. Close the final border rnd with a sl st over the first motif and fasten off. Darn in all the yarn ends.

ARMHOLES

Rejoin the yarn with a sl st at the underarm seam. Following the instructions on p. 126 for Japanese fan stitch, work 9 fan motifs around the armhole edge. Fasten off. Darn in all the yarn ends.

LOWER EDGE OF TANK TOP

Rejoin the yarn with a sl st at the left side seam. Following the instructions on p. 126 for Japanese fan stitch, work 3 rows of 8 (9) fan motifs across the front and back. Fasten off. Darn in all the yarn ends.

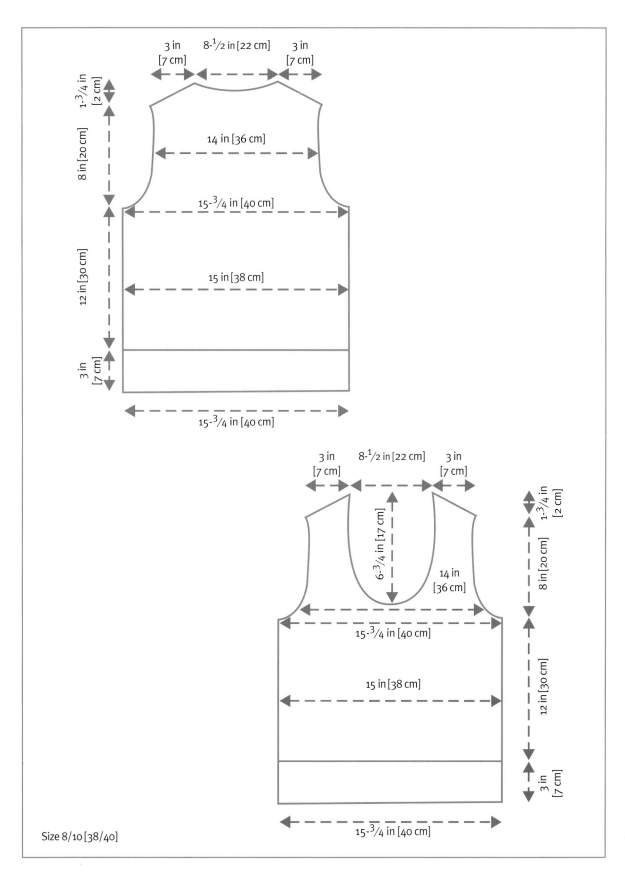

3 in [7 cm]

8-1/2 in [22 cm]

3 in [7 cm]

1-3/4 in [2 cm]

8 in [20 cm]

14 in [36 cm]

15-3/4 in [40 cm]

12 in [30 cm]

15 in [38 cm]

3 in [7 cm]

15-3/4 in [40 cm]

3 in [7 cm]

8-1/2 in [22 cm]

3 in [7 cm]

1-3/4 in [2 cm]

8 in [20 cm]

6-3/4 in [17 cm]

14 in [36 cm]

15-3/4 in [40 cm]

15 in [38 cm]

12 in [30 cm]

3 in [7 cm]

15-3/4 in [40 cm]

Size 8/10 [38/40]

5

COMPOSITES

Whether square, circle or geometric fantasy, every crochet composite starts with a central ring and is worked with the right side always facing (except for rare exceptions otherwise specified in the instructions), so there's no need to turn the work at the end of each round. Composites thus have a right side and a wrong side, something you need to be aware of when putting the various elements of a pattern together. The technique is especially interesting because, depending on the number of sections you make, you can throw a modest project together in a few hours, or spend longer and create a grand masterpiece.

WORKING IN ROUNDS

1. Work the number of ch sts specified in the instructions.

2. Join the last st to the first with a sl st to form a ring.

3. At the beginning of each round, work one or more ch sts to bring your work to the level of the stitches specified (e.g., 1 ch st equals the height of 1 sc, or 3 ch sts equal 1 double crochet).

4. In Rnd 1, work the stitches into the initial ring unless otherwise instructed. Work the number of stitches specified in the instructions.

5. To close each round, work 1 sl st over the last ch st at beg of rnd.

6–9. Beginning with Rnd 2, begin each round with 1 or more chain stitches. Insert the hook under both strands of the stitches in the preceding round.

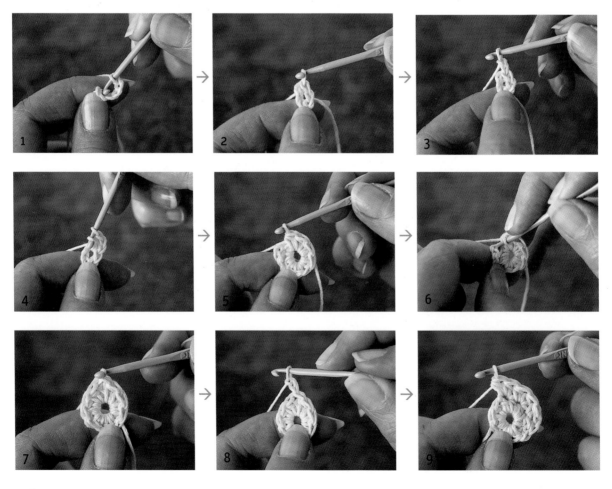

PINE CONES

Work 6 ch, join with a sl st to form a ring.

Rnd 1: 1 ch, 12 sc into ring, 1 sl st over first sc of rnd.

Rnd 2: Form a pine cone as follows: (12 ch, * 5 dc over 4th st from hook, 5 dc into each of the next 8 sts, 1 sl st in same st where you worked the initial 12 ch sts), work 1 sl st into each of the next 2 sc *, rep from * to * 5 more times. Close with a sl st (see chart).

Rnd 3: 14 ch sts, * 1 sc at tip of next pine cone, 8 ch, 1 triple tr over the sc of the rnd bet 2 pine cones, 8 ch *, rep from * to * 5 more times. End by working 8 ch, 1 sl st over the 6th of 14 ch sts at beg of rnd.

Rnd 4: 8 ch (to count as first tr tr and 2 ch sts), now work (1 tr tr, 2 ch) 4 times over same st as the 8 ch sts, * 1 sc in next sc, (1 tr tr, 2 ch) 5 times over foll tr tr *, rep from * to * 5 more times. End by working 1 sc over the next sc, 2 ch, 1 sl st over the 6th of 8 ch sts at beg of rnd.

Rnd 5: 1 ch, * 3 sc in next ch lp, 1 picot formed of 3 ch sts *, rep from * to * in each ch lp of rnd. Close with a sl st over the first sc of rnd. Fasten off.

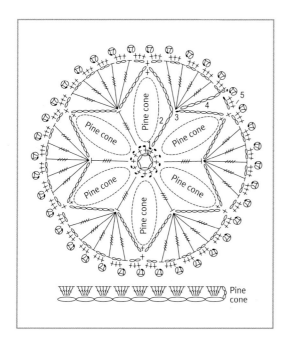

MOORISH MEDALLION

Work 6 ch, join with a sl st to form a ring.

Rnd 1: 1 ch, 16 sc into ring, 1 sl st over first sc of rnd = 16 sc.

Rnd 2: 1 ch, 1 sc in same st as ch st, 1 sc over next st, * (1 sc, 9 ch, 1 sc) once over next sc, 1 sc into each of the next 3 sc * rep from * to * to end of rnd. Close with a sl st.

Rnd 3: 1 ch, 1 sc in same st as ch st, * (2 half-dc, 17 dc, 2 half-dc) into foll ch lp, skip 2 sc, work 1 sc in foll st *, rep from * to * 3 more times. End by working 1 sl st over the sc at beg of rnd.

Rnd 4: 1 ch, over first sc work 1 elongated sc (insert the hook underneath Rnd 2, at level of Rnd 1, yo and draw up lp to height of row, yo and work 2 lps of hook), * ch, skip 5 sts, 1 sc, 3 ch, 1 sl st in 3rd ch st from hook, work (5 ch, skip 4 sts, 1 sc, 3 ch, 1 sl st in 3rd st from hook) twice, 5 ch, skip 5 sts, over foll sc work 1 elongated sc *, rep from * to * to end of rnd. Close by replacing the last elongated sc with 1 sl st over last st. Fasten off.

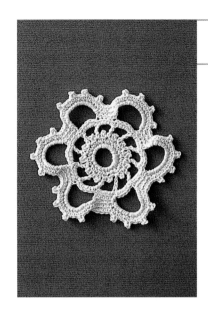

SNOW FLAKE

Work 12 ch, join with a sl st to form a ring.

Rnd 1: 1 ch, work 24 sc into ring, close with 1 sl st over first sc of rnd.

Rnd 2: 1 ch, 1 sc over same base st as ch st, 1 sc in foll st, * 1 picot formed of 3 ch, 2 sc *, rep from * to * 11 more times. After completing the 12th picot, close with 1 sl st over the sc at beg of rnd.

Rnd 3: 8 ch (to count as 1 tr plus 4 ch sts), then work * 1 tr in sc bet next 2 picots, 4 ch *, rep from * to * 10 times. After working the 11th tr, close by working 4 ch and 1 sl st over the 4th of 8 ch sts at beg of rnd.

Rnd 4: 1 ch, * 1 sc through back strand only of each of the next 5 sts, 15 ch, skip 5 sc *, rep from * to * 5 more times. End the rnd with 1 sl st over the first sc.

Rnd 5: 1 ch, * 1 sc under back strand only of each of the next 5 sc, 15 ch, skip 5 sc *, rep from * to * 5 more times. End with 1 sl st over the first sc.

Rnd 6: 1 ch, * 1 sc through back strand only of each of the next 5 sc, 15 sc into next ch lp *, rep from * to * to end. Close as before.

Rnd 7: 1 ch, 6 sc, * work (1 picot formed of 3 ch sts, 3 sc) 4 times, cont with 9 sc *, rep from * to * to end of rnd. End by working 1 sl st over the first sc. Fasten off.

TRADITIONAL HEXAGON

Work 6 ch, join with a sl st to form a ring.

Rnd 1: 3 ch, 2 dc tog into ring (to count as 3 dc tog), now work (3 ch, 3 dc tog) into ring 5 times. End the rnd by working 1 ch, 1 half-dc in top of pair of dc tog at beg of rnd.

Rnd 2: 3 ch and 2 dc tog into lp formed by half-dc (to count as 3 dc tog), then into foll ch lp work * 3 ch, (3 dc tog, 3 ch, 3 dc tog) *, rep from * to * 4 more times. End by working 3 ch, 3 dc tog in last ch lp and 1 ch, then 1 half-dc in top of 2 dc tog at beg of rnd.

Rnd 3: 3 ch, 2 dc tog in lp formed by half- dc (to count as 3 dc tog), then * work 3 ch, into foll ch lp (3 dc tog, 3 ch, 3 dc tog), 3 ch, 3 dc tog in foll ch lp *, rep from * to * 4 more times. Close with 3 ch, (3 dc tog, 3 ch, 3 dc tog) in foll lp, 1 ch and 1 half-dc in top of 2 dc tog at beg of rnd.

Rnd 4: 3 ch (to count as first dc), 1 dc in lp formed by half-dc, * 3 dc in next ch lp, into foll ch lp work (3 dc, 2 ch, 3 dc), 3 dc in next lp *, rep from * to * 5 more times. End by working 1 dc into the last lp followed by 1 sl st in the 3rd ch st at beg of rnd.

Rnd 5: 1 ch, 1 sc in same st as ch st just worked, then 1 sc in each dc and in each ch st of the rnd. End with 1 sl st over the first sc at beg of rnd. Fasten off.

RAISED HEXAGON

Work 4 ch, join with a sl st to form a ring.

Rnd 1: 3 ch (to count as first dc), then into ring work (1 ch, 2 dc) 5 times. End the rnd by working 1 ch, 1 sl st in 3rd ch st at beg of rnd (= 6 sides).

Rnd 2: 1 sl st over each of first 2 sts, 3 ch (to count as 1 dc), * 2 dc through back strand only of st in previous rnd, then into next ch lp work (1 dc, 1 ch, 1 dc)*, rep from * to * 5 more times. End by working 1 dc in the last ch lp, 1 ch, and 1 sl st in 3rd ch st at beg of rnd.

Rnd 3: 3 ch, (to count as 1 dc), then * work 1 dc through back strand only of each dc in the preceding rnd, and at each corner work (1 dc, 1 ch, 1 dc) *. End the rnd by working 1 sl st in 3rd ch st at beg of rnd. You have a hexagon with 6 dc on each side.

Rnd 4: Repeat Rnd 3. End with 1 sl st in the 3rd of 3 ch sts at beg of rnd. You now have a hexagon with 8 dc on each side.

Rnd 5: Repeat Rnd 3. End with 1 sl st in the 3rd of 3 ch sts at beg of rnd. You now have a hexagon with 10 dc on each side. Fasten off.

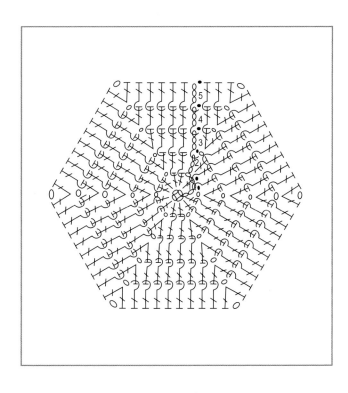

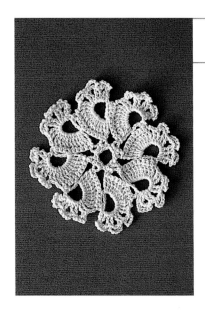

CURLICUE

Work this composite petal by petal, forming the central ring as the last step.

For petal 1, work 12 ch, join with a sl st to form a ring.

Rnd 1 (rs): 4 ch (to count as first tr), now working into the ring cont with (1 tr, 6 ch, 1 dc at top of preceding tr, 1 tr) 3 times, 1 tr, 2 ch, 10 tr. Turn the work.

Rnd 2: 5 ch, 1 sl st in 5th st from hook, * skip the first tr, work 1 sc over each of the next 9 tr. Turn the work.

Rnd 3 (petal 2): 1 ch, 1 sc in same st as ch st just worked, 3 ch, skip 3 sc along the edge of the preceding petal, work 1 sc in next st, 9 ch, 1 sl st into the first sc to complete the ring of the 2nd petal.

Rnd 4: Repeat Rnd 1.

Rnd 5: Repeat Rnd 2.

Rnd 6 (next petal): 2 ch, 1 sc in picot of preceding petal, 3 ch, 1 sl st in first ch st of row to complete the picot, then cont as for petal 1, beg with *.

Complete 5 more petals, repeating from * to *. End the 8th petal as follows: 2 ch, 1 sc in picot of 7th petal, 1 ch, 1 sc in picot of first petal (this closes the motif in a circle), 2 ch, 1 sl st in first ch st to complete the picot, skip the first tr, work 1 sc in each of the next 5 tr, work 1 sl st in the first petal, 1 sc over each of the next 4 tr, 1 sl st in the loop of the first petal. Fasten off.

Central ring: Rejoin the yarn with a sl st in an sc at the center of the petals (see chart) and work as follows: 1 ch, 1 sc in same st as ch st just worked, now work (1 sc in next picot, 1 sc sideways on foll sc) 7 times, 1 sc in next picot, 1 sl st in first sc at beg of rnd. Fasten off.

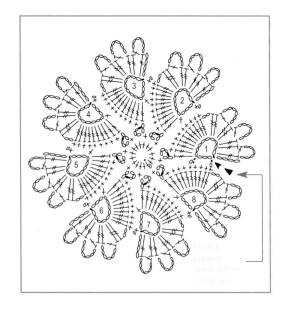

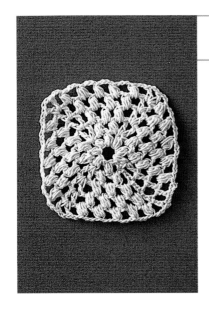

HAWAIIAN SQUARE

Work 8 ch and join with a sl st to form a ring.

Rnd 1: 2 ch, and working into ring cont with 1 puff st formed of 4 half-dc (count as 1 puff st formed of 5 half-dc), 2 ch, then (1 puff st formed of 5 half-dc, 2 ch) 7 times. End the rnd by working 1 sl st in the top of the first puff st.

Rnd 2: 5 ch (= 1 half-dc and 2 ch sts), 1 dc over first puff st, * 2 ch, the (1 puff st formed of 5 half-dc in next ch lp, 2 ch) twice, and form the corner loop by working (1 dc, 2 ch 1 dc) over the following puff st *. Repeat from * to * twice more. End rnd by working (2 ch, 1 puff st in foll ch lp) twice, 2 ch, and 1 sl st in 3rd of 5 ch sts at beg of rnd.

Rnd 3: 1 sl st in next ch st, 5 ch (= 1 dc and 2 ch), 1 dc in same corner ch lp, * 2 ch, (1 puff st formed of 5 half-dc in foll ch lp, 2 ch) 3 times, and at corner work 1 dc, 2 ch, and 1 dc *. Rep from * to * twice more. End the rnd by working (2 ch, 1 puff st in foll ch lp) 3 times, 2 ch, and 1 sl st over the 3rd of 5 ch sts at beg of rnd.

Rnd 4: 1 sl st in next ch st, 5 ch (= 1 dc and 2 ch), 1 dc in same corner ch lp, * 2 ch, (1 puff st formed of 5 half-dc in foll ch lp, 2 ch) 4 times, and at corner work 1 dc, 2 ch, and 1 dc *. Rep from * to * twice more. End the rnd by working (2 ch, 1 puff st in foll ch lp) 4 times, 2 ch, and 1 sl st over the 3rd of 5 ch sts at beg of rnd.

Rnd 5: 1 sl st in next ch st, 5 ch (= 1 dc and 2 ch), 1 dc in same corner ch lp, * 2 ch, (1 puff st formed of 5 half-dc in foll ch lp, 2 ch) 5 times, and at corner work 1 dc, 2 ch, and 1 dc *. Rep from * to * twice more. End the rnd by working (2 ch, 1 puff st in foll ch lp) 5 times, 2 ch, and 1 sl st over the 3rd of 5 ch sts at beg of rnd.
Fasten off.

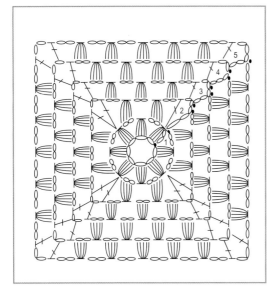

STARRY SQUARE

Work 12 ch and join with a sl st to form a ring.

Rnd 1: 1 ch, then into ring work 24 sc; close with a sl st over the first sc of rnd = 24 sc.

Rnd 2: 6 ch, 3 dbl tr tog over the next 3 sts (counts as 4 dbl tr tog), now work (7 ch, 4 dbl tr tog, working the first over the preceding st then over the next 3 sts) 7 times. End by working 7 ch followed by 1 sl st in the top of the first group of sts tog.

Rnd 3: 1 ch, 1 sc in same st as ch st just worked, * work (3 ch, skip 1 ch st, 1 sc over foll ch st) 3 times, 3 ch, 1 sc in top of next group of sts tog *, rep from * to * 7 more times. At the end of the rnd, replace the last sc with 1 sl st over the first sc at beg of rnd.

Rnds 4 and 5: 1 sl st over each of the first 2 ch sts, 1 ch, 1 sc in same ch lp, * 3 ch, 1 sc in next ch lp *, rep from * to * to end. At the end of the rnd, replace the last sc with 1 sl st over the sc at beg of rnd.

Rnd 6: Work forward with a sl st over each of the next 2 sts, 1 ch, 1 sc in same ch lp, * in foll ch lp work (3 ch, 1 sc in next ch lp) 4 times, 3 ch, skip 1 ch lp, then work (3 tr tog, 5 ch, 4 dbl tr tog, 4 ch, 1 sl st in the top of the group just worked, 5 ch, 3 tr tog) *, rep from * to * to end of rnd. At the end of the rnd, replace the last sc with 1 sl st over the sc at beg of rnd. Fasten off.

BALTIC SQUARE

Work 8 ch and join with a sl st to form a ring.

Rnd 1: 3 ch, then working into ring cont with 1 cluster of 4 dc (counts as a cluster made up of 5 dc), then work (5 ch, 1 5-dc cluster) 3 times. End the rnd with 5 ch followed by a sl st in the top of the first cluster.

Rnd 2: 3 ch (= 1 dc), * in next ch lp work (2 dc, 2 ch, 1 5-dc cluster, 2 ch, 2 dc), and work 1 5-dc cluster over the next cluster of the previous row *. Repeat from * to * twice more. End the rnd by working 2 dc, 2 ch, 1 5-dc cluster, 2 ch, 2 dc, and 1 sl st over the 3rd ch st at beg of rnd.

Rnd 3: 3 ch (= 1 dc), 2 dc, * work 2 dc in next ch lp, 2 ch, 1 5-dc cluster over following cluster, 2 ch, 2 dc in next ch lp, 5 dc *. Rep from * to * twice more. End the rnd by working 2 dc in the next ch lp, 2 ch, 1 5-dc cluster over the foll cluster, 2 ch, 2 dc in last ch lp, 1 sl st in 3rd ch st at beg of rnd.

Rnd 4: 3 ch (= 1 dc), 4 dc, * work 2 dc in next ch lp, 2 ch, 1 5-dc cluster over following cluster, 2 ch, 2 dc in next ch lp, 9 dc *. Rep from * to * twice more. End the rnd by working 2 dc in the next ch lp, 2 ch, 1 5-dc cluster over the foll cluster, 2 ch, 2 dc in next ch lp, 4 dc in last ch lp, 1 sl st in 3rd ch st at beg of rnd. Fasten off.

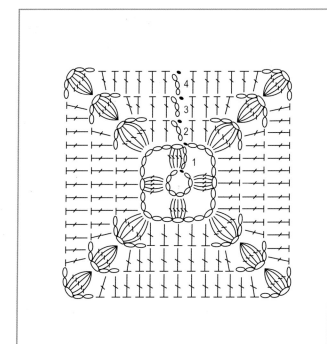

DAISY

Work 10 ch, join with a sl st to form a ring.

Rnd 1: 1 ch (to count as 1 sc), and into ring work 17 sc (= 18 sc). End the rnd by working 1 sl st over the ch st at beg.

Rnd 2: 1 ch (to count as 1 sc), * 1 sc over each of next 3 sc, 2 sc in foll sc *, rep from * to * 4 times (= 24 sc). End the rnd by working 1 sl st over the ch st at beg.

Rnd 3: 1 ch (to count as 1 sc), * 2 sc over next sc, 1 sc in each of the 4 foll sc *, rep from * to * 4 times (= 29 sc). End the rnd by working 1 sl st over the ch st at beg.

Rnd 4: 1 ch (to count as 1 sc), * 1 sc over each of next 5 sc, 2 sc in foll sc *, rep from * to * 4 times (= 34 sc). End the rnd by working 1 sl st over the ch st at beg.

Rnd 5: 1 ch (to count as 1 sc), * 2 sc over next sc, 1 sc in each of the 6 foll sc *, rep from * to * 4 times (= 39 sc). End the rnd by working 1 sl st over the ch st at beg.

Rnd 6: 1 ch (to count as 1 sc), * 1 sc, 9 ch, skip 4 sc *, rep from * to * 7 times. End the rnd by working 1 sl st over the ch st at beg.

Rnd 7: 1 ch (= 1 sc), then work 17 sc in each 10-st ch lp of preceding rnd. End the rnd by working 1 sl st over the ch st at beg. Fasten off.

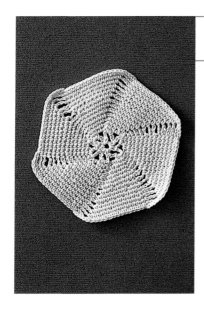

WINDMILL

Work 5 ch and join with a sl st to form a ring.

Rnd 1: 1 ch (counts as first dc of rnd), 6 ch, into ring work * 1 sc, 6 ch *, rep from * to * 4 times. End by working 1 sl st over ch st at beg of rnd.

Rnd 2: Work forward with a sl st in each of the first 4 sts of first ch lp, 1 ch (to count as first sc), 1 sc in first ch lp, * 4 ch, 2 sc in next ch lp *, rep from * to * 4 times. End by working 4 ch, 1 sc in first ch lp and 1 sl st in ch st at beg of rnd.

Rnd 3: 1 ch (to count as first sc), * 4 ch, 1 sc in next 4-st ch lp, 1 sc over each of the foll 2 sc *, rep from * to * 4 times. End by working 4 ch, 1 sc in next ch lp and 1 sl st in ch st at beg of rnd.

Rnds 4–9: Repeat Rnd 3, adding 1 extra st to each vane of the windmill with each successive round.

Rnds 10–16: As for Rnds 4–9, working 5 ch sts bet the vanes of the windmill (see chart). At the completion of Rnd 16, fasten off.

WHIRLPOOL

This pattern is worked in a spiral, without closing off each rnd. To make your work easier, attach a safety pin or a contrasting yarn marker to indicate the last sc of each round.

Work 5 ch and join with a sl st to form a ring.

Rnd 1: Into ring work (6 ch, 1 sc) 5 times.

Rnd 2: Into ring work (6 ch, 3 sc) 5 times.

Rnd 3: Work (6 ch, 3 sc in foll ch lp, 2 sc) 5 times = 5 groups of 5 sc.

Rnd 4: Work (6 ch, 3 sc in foll ch lp, 1 sc in each sc of foll group except the last sc) 5 times = 5 groups of 7 sc.

Rnd 5: Work (6 ch, 3 sc in foll ch lp, 1 sc in each sc of foll group except the last sc) 5 times = 5 groups of 9 sc.

Rnd 6: Work (6 ch, 3 sc in foll ch lp, 1 sc in each sc of foll group except the last sc) 5 times = 5 groups of 11 sc.

Rnd 7: Work (6 ch, 3 sc in foll ch lp, 1 sc in each sc of foll group except the last sc) 5 times = 5 groups of 13 sc.

Rnd 8: * 5 ch, 1 sc at center of foll ch lp, 5 ch, skip 1 sc, work 1 sc in each sc of foll group except the last sc *, rep from * to * 4 more times.

Rnd 9: * (5 ch, 1 sc in foll ch lp) twice, 5 ch, skip 1 sc, work 1 sc in each sc of foll group except the last sc *, rep from * to * 4 more times.

Rnd 10: * (5 ch, 1 sc in foll ch lp) 3 times, 5 ch, skip 1 sc, work 1 sc in each sc of foll group except the last sc *, rep from * to * 4 more times.

Rnd 11: * (5 ch, 1 sc in foll ch lp) 4 times, 5 ch, skip 1 sc, work 1 sc in each sc of foll group except the last sc *, rep from * to * 4 more times.

Rnd 12: * (5 ch, 1 sc in foll ch lp) 5 times, 5 ch, skip 1 sc, work 1 sc in each sc of foll group except the last sc *, rep from * to * 4 more times.

Rnd 13: 5 ch, 1 sc in foll ch lp, * (3 ch, 1 sc in foll ch lp) 5 times, 3 ch, skip 1 sc, 1 dc, 3 ch in next ch lp *, rep from * to * 4 more times.

At end of rnd, replace the last sc with a sl st over the first sc of rnd.

Fasten off.

WHEEL

Work this composite section by section counterclockwise around the central ring that is formed at the same time as the first section.

Section 1: Work 17 ch sts, 1 sl st in 8th st from hook, 1 sc in next ch st, following the chart, in the foll ch sts work 1 half-dc, 1 dc, 2 dc, 2 tr in foll ch st, 1 tr, 2 dbl tr in next sts, and 1 dbl tr in foll st.

Do not turn the work. Continue by working 1 sc from left to right (see crab stitch technique on p. 45) through front strand only of each of the sts just worked. End by working 1 sl st in the ring formed at beg of section 1.

Section 2: Working through back strand only of sts, just behind the crab stitch work 1 half-dc, 1 dc, 2 dc in foll st, 2 tr in foll ch st, 1 tr, 2 dbl tr in next sts, and 1 dbl tr in foll st. As for section 1, do not turn the work, but continue with 1 row of crab stitch. End by working 1 sl st in the ring formed at beg of section 1.

Sections 3–10: As given for section 2.

At completion of section 10, fasten off, leaving a length of about 10 in [25 cm]. Sew section 10 to section 1.

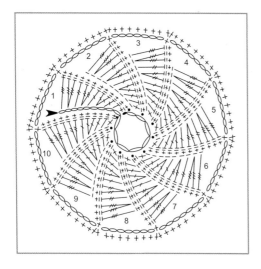

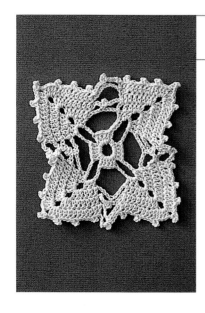

CRYSTAL SQUARE

Work 10 ch, join with a sl st to form a ring.

Rnd 1: Work 14 ch, then into ring work (5 dc, 11 ch) 3 times, followed by 4 dc. End the rnd by working 1 sl st in the 3rd of 14 ch sts at beg of rnd.

Rnd 2: 1 sl st in 5th foll ch st (see chart), 3 ch (count as first dc), then work (2 dc, 3 ch, 3 dc) in first ch lp, * 9 ch, (3 dc, 3 ch, 3 dc) in next ch lp *, rep from * to * twice more. End by working 9 ch and 1 sl st into the 3rd ch st at beg of rnd.

Rnd 3: 3 ch (= 1 dc), 2 dc, * in foll ch lp work (3 dc , 3 ch, 3 dc), 3 dc, 5 ch, skip 4 sts, 1 sc and 1 picot formed of 3 ch in foll ch st (see chart), 5 ch, skip next 4 ch sts, 3 dc *. Rep from * to * twice more. End by working (3 dc, 3 ch, 3 dc) in next ch lp, 3 dc, 5 ch, skip 4 ch sts, 1 sc and 1 3-st picot in foll ch st, 5 ch, and 1 sl st over the 3rd ch st at beg of rnd.

Rnd 4: 3 ch, 5 dc, * in next ch lp work (3 dc, 3 ch, 3 dc), 6 dc, 10 ch, skip 2 ch lps of the preceding rnd, 1 dc in each of next 6 dc *. Rep from * to * twice more. End by working (3 dc, 3 ch, 3 dc) in next ch lp, 6 dc, 10 ch, skip 2 ch lps of previous rnd, and work 1 sl st in 3rd ch st at beg of rnd.

Rnd 5: 6 ch, 1 sl st in 4th st from hook (= 1 dc + 1 picot), then work * (4 dc, 1 picot formed of 3 ch sts) twice, into foll ch lp work (3 dc, 5 ch, 1 sl st in 4th st from hook, 1 ch, 3 dc), 1 dc, 1 3-st picot, work (4 dc, 1 picot) twice, 4 ch, skip 4 sts, in 5th ch st work (1 sc, 1 picot), 4 ch, 1 dc over foll dc, 1 picot *. Repeat from * to * twice more. End by working (3 dc, 5 ch, 3 dc) in next ch lp, 1 dc, 1 3-st picot, (4 dc, 1 picot) twice, 1 dc, 4 ch, skip 4 sts, in 5th ch st work (1 sc, 1 picot), 4 ch and 1 sl st in 3rd ch st at beg of rnd. Fasten off.

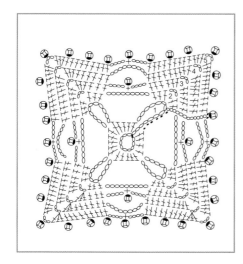

DOUBLE CROCHET SQUARE

Work 4 ch and join with a sl st to form a ring.

Rnd 1: 5 ch (to count as 1 dc + 2 ch), working into ring cont with (3 dc, 2 ch) 3 times. End by working 2 dc and 1 sl st in the 3rd of 5 ch sts at beg of rnd.

Rnd 2: Work forward with 1 sl st in next ch st, 7 ch (= 1 dc + 4 ch), into same ch lp work * 2 dc, 1 dc over each foll dc to form the side of the square, 2 dc into foll ch lp, 4 ch *, rep from * to * 3 more times. End by working only 1 dc into first ch lp, 1 sl st over 3rd of 7 ch sts at beg of rnd.

Rnd 3: Work forward with 1 sl st in next ch st, 7 ch (= 1 dc + 4 ch), into same ch lp work * 2 dc, 1 dc over each of the foll 7 dc for the side of the square, 2 dc into foll ch lp, 4 ch *, rep from * to * 3 more times. End by working only 1 dc into first ch lp, 1 sl st over 3rd of 7 ch sts at beg of rnd.

Rnd 4: Work forward with 1 sl st in next ch st, 7 ch (= 1 dc + 4 ch), into same ch lp work * 2 dc, 1 dc over each of the foll 11 dc for the side of the square, 2 dc into foll ch lp, 4 ch *, rep from * to * 3 more times. End by working only 1 dc into first ch lp, 1 sl st over 3rd of 7 ch sts at beg of rnd. Fasten off.

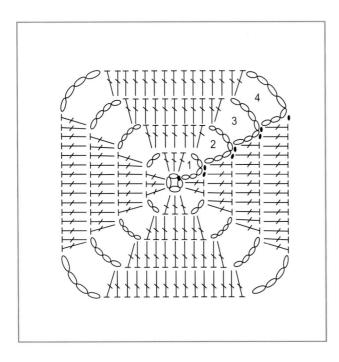

OLD AMERICA SQUARE

Work 4 ch and join with a sl st to form a ring.

Rnd 1: 3 ch (to count as first dc), then work * 2 ch, 3 dc into ring *, rep from * to * twice. End by working 2 ch, 2 dc and 1 sl st into 3rd ch st at beg of rnd.

Rnd 2: 3 ch (to count as first dc), then work 2 ch, 3 dc into first 2-st ch lp of preceding rnd, * 1 ch, and in foll 2-st ch lp work (3 dc, 2 ch, 3 dc) *, rep from * to * twice and end by working 1 ch, 2 dc in first ch lp of rnd, 1 sl st in 3rd ch st at beg of rnd.

Rnd 3: 3 ch (to count as first dc), then work 2 ch, 3 dc into first 2-st ch lp of preceding rnd, * 1 ch, 3 dc in foll 1-st ch lp, and in next lp work (3 dc, 2 ch, 3 dc) *, rep from * to * twice and end by working 1 ch, 3 dc in next 1-st ch lp, 2 dc in first ch lp of rnd, and 1 sl st in 3rd ch st at beg of rnd.

Rnd 4: 3 ch (to count as first dc), then work 2 ch, 3 dc into first 2-st ch lp of preceding rnd, * (1 ch, 3 dc in foll 1-st ch lp) twice, and in next lp work (3 dc, 2 ch, 3 dc) *, rep from * to * twice and end by working 1 ch,(3 dc in next 1-st ch lp) twice, 2 dc in first ch lp of rnd, and 1 sl st in 3rd ch st at beg of rnd.

Fasten off.

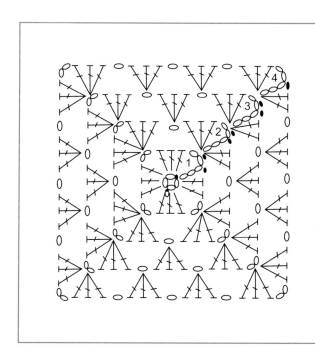

ROSY SQUARE

Work 8 ch and join with a sl st to form a ring.

Rnd 1: 1 ch, into ring work 18 sc, close with 1 sl st over first ch st of rnd.

Rnd 2: 1 ch, beg in same st as ch st work * 1 sc, 3 ch, skip 2 sts *, rep from * to * 5 times. End by working 1 sl st over first sc of rnd.

Rnd 3: 1 ch, work 1 petal as follows, (1 sc, 1 ch, 5 dc, 3 ch, 1 sc) into each of the foll 6 ch lps of the preceding rnd. End by working 1 sl st over first sc of rnd.

Rnd 4: 1 ch, then *1 sc bet 2 sc, fold the petal of Rnd 3 forward and work 5 ch sts behind it *, rep from * to * 5 times. End by working 1 sl st over the first sc of rnd.

Rnd 5: 1 ch, then work 1 petal (1 sc, 3 ch, 7 dc, 3 ch, 1 sc) in each of the 6 ch lps of Rnd 4. End by working 1 sl st over first sc of rnd.

Rnd 6: 1 ch, then *1 sc bet 2 sc, fold the petal of Rnd 3 forward and work 7 ch sts behind it *, rep from * to * 5 times. End by working 1 sl st over the first sc of rnd.

Rnd 7: 1 sl st in next ch st, 3 ch (= 1 dc), then (4 dc, 2 ch, 1 dc) in first ch lp. Continue with * 6 dc in next ch lp, then (2 dc, 2 ch, 4 dc) in foll ch lp *, followed by (5 dc, 2 ch, 1 dc) in next ch lp, rep from * to * once. End by working 1 sl st over 3rd ch st at beg of rnd.

Rnd 8: 3 ch (= 1 dc), work, 1 dc over each dc and, in each corner lp work (3 dc, 2 ch, 3 dc). End by working 1 sl st over 3rd ch st at beg of rnd.

Rnd 9: 3 ch (= 1 dc), work 1 dc over each dc and, in each corner lp work (2 dc, 2 ch, 2 dc). End by working 1 sl st over 3rd ch st at beg of rnd. Fasten off.

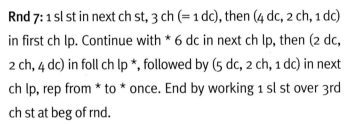

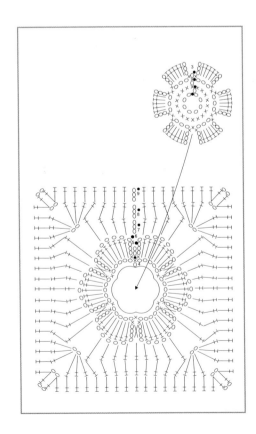

Accent pillow

ACCENT PILLOW

Materials

5 50g balls of Gedifra "Korella" (53% linen, 47% acrylic)

Mauve no. 8435.

1 3 mm crochet hook

1 darning or tapestry needle

1 sewing needle

Woven linen fabric in Prince of Wales check, mauve background, measuring approximately 14-$\frac{1}{2}$ X 28-$\frac{1}{2}$ in [37 X 72 cm].

mauve sewing thread

1 crewel needle

pins

synthetic batting

Size

Each Baltic square measures approximately 3 in [8 cm] on a side

Finished pillow measures approximately 13-$\frac{3}{4}$ in [35 cm] on a side.

Stitches used

Baltic square (p. 169)

Skill level

* Beginner

TO MAKE

Following the directions on p. 169, complete 36 identical Baltic squares and darn in all the yarn ends. Place 2 squares rs tog and join by backstitching, then join the remaining squares until you have a rectangle measuring approximately 12-$\frac{1}{2}$ X 28-$\frac{1}{2}$ in [32 X 72 cm], as indicated in the chart on p. 180.

Center the crocheted band on the linen fabric and slipstitch the 4 sides, using the crewel needle and the sewing thread.

ASSEMBLY

Overcast the raw edge of the linen. Fold the rectangle in half rs tog and stitch $\frac{1}{2}$ in [1 cm] from the edge across one length and one width (see chart).

Fold the rectangle in half again, overlapping points A and B as shown in the chart. Stitch B to C and C to E'. One side of the pillow cover remains open. Spread it so as to place the seam to AB to E at the center of the edge that remains to be sewn. Stitch halfway along the seam.

Press the seams open and turn the pillow right side out. Stuff the pillow with synthetic batting, making sure that the corners are well filled. Slipstitch the rest of the seam by hand.

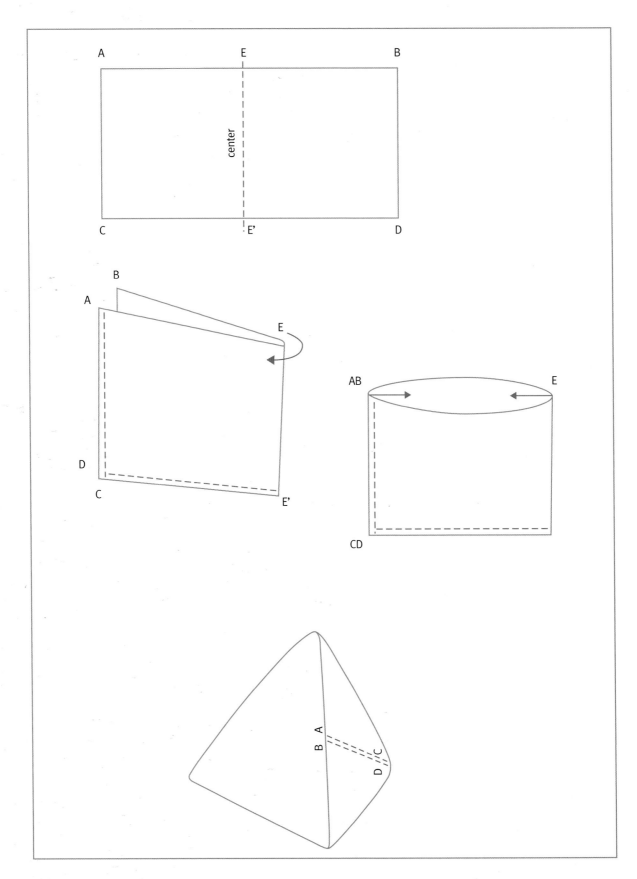

Lampshade

LAMPSHADE

Materials

1 50g ball each in Coats "Aïda" (100% cotton) in White, Ecru no. 926, Grège no. 387, Ficelle no. 842

1 1.75 mm crochet hook

1 darning or tapestry needle

1 white lampshade 6 in [15 cm] in diameter and 8 in [20 cm] tall.

1 tube of fabric glue

pins

Size

Finished lampshade measures 6 X 8 in [15 X 20 cm]

Stitches used

Double crochet square (p. 176)

Snow flake (p. 163)

Single crochet (p. 47)

Daisy (p. 170)

Moorish medallion (p. 162)

Skill level

** Some experience

TO MAKE

Complete 5 double crochet squares, working Rnds 1, 2, and 4 in white and Rnd 3 in gray-beige (Grège).

Complete 5 daisies, working Rnds 1–5 in string color (Ficelle), and Rnds 6 and 7 in ecru.

Complete 12 Moorish medallions, including 4 white, 4 ecru, and 4 string color (Ficelle).

Complete 5 snow flakes, working Rnds 1–4 in white and Rnds 5–7 in string color (Ficelle).

Darn in the yarn ends as you complete each composite.

ASSEMBLY

Arrange the composites on the lampshade, using pins to hold them in place. When you are satisfied with the arrangement, coat the back of each composite with a thin coat of fabric glue and attach it to the lampshade.

FINISHING

You may find that you have rather wide spaces left between some of the composites. Fill them by working remnants of white cotton into circles of single crochets (see p. 184), as shown in the photo.

CIRCLES IN SINGLE CROCHET

Work 4 ch and join with a sl st to form a ring.

Rnd 1: 1 ch, then work 8 sc into ring. Close with a sl st over the ch st at beg of rnd.

Rnd 2: 1 ch, 1 sc into foll st, then 2 sc into each of the next 7 sts = 16 sts. Close the rnd with a sl st over the ch st at beg of rnd.

Rnd 3: 1 ch, 1 sc into next st, then * 2 sc in next st and 1 sc in foll st *. Rep from * to * to end of rnd = 24 sts. Close with a sl st over the ch st at beg of rnd.

Rnd 4: 1 ch, 1 sc into next st, then * 2 sc in next st and 1 sc in each of foll 2 sts *. Rep from * to * to end of rnd. Close with a sl st over the ch st at beg of rnd.

Rnd 5: 1 ch, 1 sc into next st, then * 2 sc in next st and 1 sc into each of foll 3 sts *. Rep from * to * to end of rnd. Close with a sl st over the ch st at beg of rnd.

Rnd 6: 1 ch, 1 sc into next st, then * 2 sc in next st and 1 sc into each of foll 4 sts *. Rep from * to * to end of rnd. Close with a sl st over the ch st at beg of rnd.

Complete as many rounds as necessary to fill in the gap. Glue the completed circles between the previously applied composites.

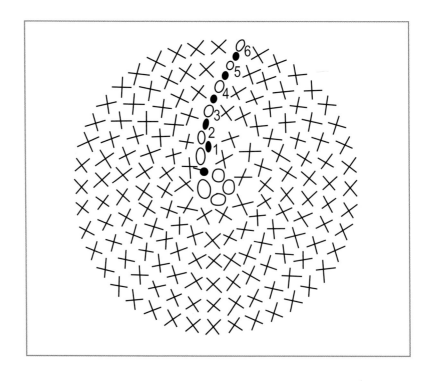

Afghan

Materials

2 50g balls each in Rowan "Felted Tweed" (50% merino wool, 25% alpaca, 25% viscose) in the following colors:

A Cocoa no. 143, B Dragon no. 147, C Ginger no.154, D Rage no. 150, E Bilberry no. 151, F Herb no. 146

1 3.5 mm crochet hook

1 darning or tapestry needle

Size

Each double crochet square measures approximately 3-1/4 in [8 cm] on a side.

Finished afghan measures 33-1/2 in [85 cm] square.

Stitches used

Double crochets (p. 49)

Double crochet square (p. 176)

Skill level

* Beginner

TO MAKE

Following the indications for colors A–F in the chart on p. 186, complete 100 double crochet squares. Darn in all the yarn ends, then join the squares, rs tog, by backstitching the seams.

FINISHING

Work 2 bands each in brown (A, Cocoa) and gray (B, Dragon), as follows. Work 194 ch sts for a base chain. Rows 1–3: 3 ch (= first dc of row, then work 1 dc over each st of preceding row). At completion of Row 3, fasten off and darn in the yarn ends.

Backstitch the borders to the rest of the afghan, alternating gray and brown, and staggering the colors at the corners. as shown in the photo.

A

A	B	C	D	E	F	A	B	C	D
F	A	B	C	D	E	F	A	B	C
E	F	A	B	C	D	E	F	A	B
D	E	F	A	B	C	D	E	F	A
C	D	E	F	A	B	C	D	E	F
B	C	D	E	F	A	B	C	D	E
A	B	C	D	E	F	A	B	C	D
F	A	B	C	D	E	F	A	B	C
E	F	A	B	C	D	E	F	A	B
D	E	F	A	B	C	D	E	F	A

F (left)   F (right)

A

A = Cocoa 143
B = Dragon 147
C = Ginger 154
D = Rage 150
E = Billberry 151
F = Herb 146

Brooches

BROOCHES

Materials

1 25g ball each in Gedifra "Easy Soft" (48% mohair, 42% polyamide, 10% cashmere) in the following colors:

Vert no. 8607, Orange no. 8621, Bleu no. 8680

1 1.75 mm crochet hook

1 crewel needle

2 brooch fasteners

Sewing thread

Size

Each finished brooch measures approximately 4-³/₄ in [12 cm] in diameter.

Stitches used

Double crochets (p. 42)

Moorish medallion (p. 162) with added stitches

Skill level

* Beginner

TO MAKE

Using blue or green, work 6 ch, join with a sl st to form a ring.

Rnd 1: 3 ch (= first dc), then into ring work 29 dc; close with a sl st in 3rd ch st at beg of rnd = 30 dc. Fasten off.

Rnd 2: Using green or orange, work 9 ch, 1 sc over first st, then 1 sc in each of the next 2 sts, * 9 ch, 1 sc in each of next 3 sts *, rep from * to * to end of rnd. Close by working 1 sl st at base of the 9 ch sts at beg of rnd (= 10 ch lps).

Rnd 3: * In foll 9-st ch lp work 2 sc, 3 half-dc, 5 dc, 1 picot formed of 3 ch sts, 5 dc, 3 half-dc, 2 sc, then skip 1 sc of preceding rnd and work 1 sc in foll st, skip next sc *, rep from * to * to end of round, forming 10 petals.

Rnd 4: * 7 ch, slip the chain thus formed behind the next petal, work 1 sc over sc bet 2 petals in preceding rnd , 9 ch, 1 sc in same base st *, rep from * to * to end of rnd, forming a second row of 10 petals.

Rnd 5: * 5 sc in 7-st ch lp, the in foll 9-st ch lp form a petal as follows: 2 sc, 3 half-dc, 5 dc, 1 picot formed of 3 ch sts, 5 dc, 3 half-dc, 2 sc *. Rep from * to * to end of rnd. Close the end with 1 sl st over the first sc of rnd. Fasten off.

FINISHING

Darn in all the yarn ends. Attach the brooch fastener to the wrong side of the flower with a few little stitches.

Belt

BELT

Materials

1 50g ball each in Coats "Aïda" (100% cotton) yarn in the following colors:

Aubergine no. 1028, Bordeaux no. 47, and Orange no. 8621

1 1.75 mm crochet hook

1 darning or tapestry needle

1 metal belt buckle measuring 3-3/4 X 2-3/4 in [9.5 X 7 cm]

Size

Finished belt measures approximately 29-1/2 X 2-3/4 in [75 X 7.5 cm].

Stitches used

Old America squares (p. 177)

Single crochets (p. 47)

Skill level

* Beginner

TO MAKE

Complete 12 Old America squares (see p. 177) in each of 3 different color combinations:

A: Rnd 1 Aubergine, Rnd 2 Bordeaux, Rnd 3 Orange.
B: Rnd 1 Bordeaux, Rnd 2 Orange, Rnd 3 Aubergine.
C: Rnd 1 Orange, Rnd 2 Aubergine, Rnd 3 Bordeaux.

ASSEMBLY

Darn in all the yarn ends. Following the indications for colors in the chart below, place the squares rs tog and join them by backstitching. Press the completed belt band, ws facing, under a damp cloth.

FINISHING

Join the Bordeaux yarn with a sl st at one end of the belt and work 1 row of sc on all 4 sides. At one end, fold 2 cm to the ws over the prongs of the belt buckle. Slipstitch the fold on ws of belt.

A	B	C	A	B	C	A	B	C	A	B	C	A	B	C	A	B
C	A	B	C	A	B	C	A	B	C	A	B	C	A	B	C	A

6
INDEXES

Stitches

double crochet
p. 42, 49

raised double crochet through
back strand of sts
p. 91

raised double crochet through front
strand of sts
p. 91

crossed double crochets
p. 94

shells
p. 122

horizontal ribbing
p. 90

half-double crochet
p. 41

treble crochet
p.43

bundle
p. 124

chain stitch
p. 24

slip stitch
p. 41

single crochet
p. 40, 47

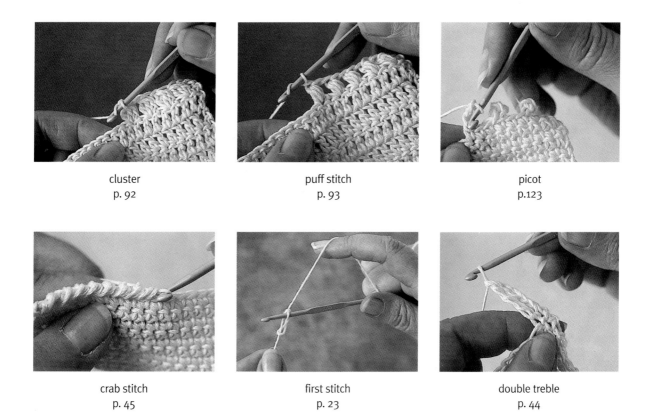

cluster
p. 92

puff stitch
p. 93

picot
p.123

crab stitch
p. 45

first stitch
p. 23

double treble
p. 44

Pattern stitches

crowned loops
p. 140

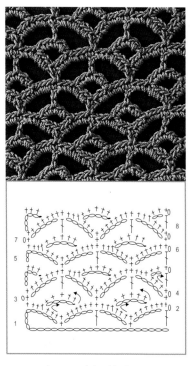

staggered double loops
p. 138

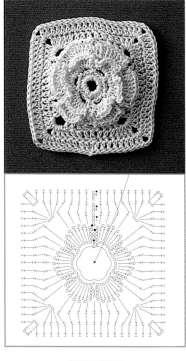

rosy square
p. 178

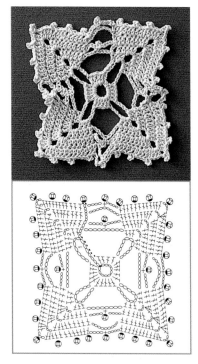

crystal square
p. 175

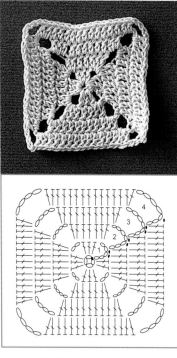

double crochet square
p. 176

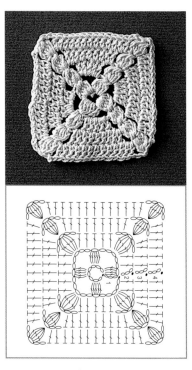

Baltic square
p. 169

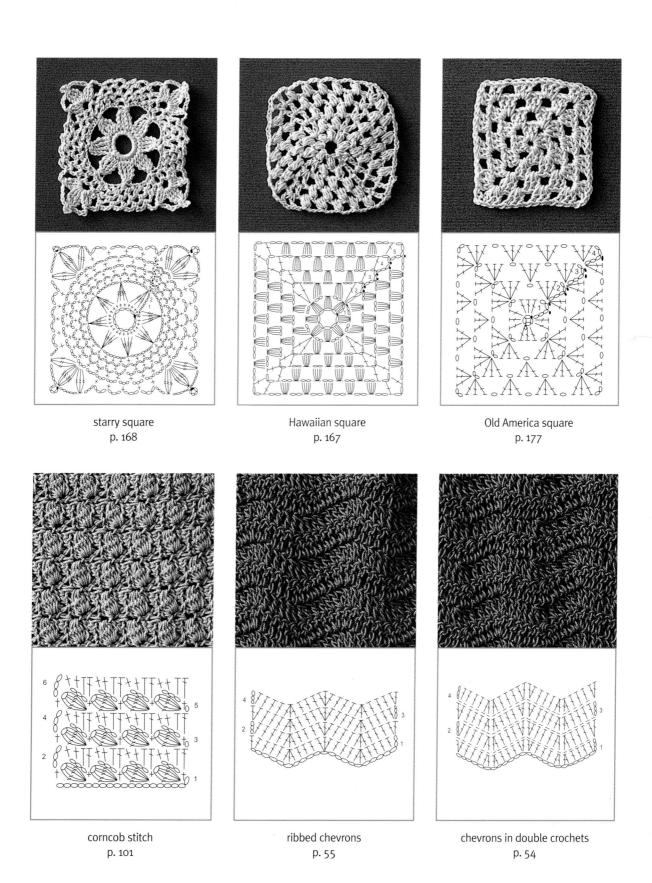

starry square
p. 168

Hawaiian square
p. 167

Old America square
p. 177

corncob stitch
p. 101

ribbed chevrons
p. 55

chevrons in double crochets
p. 54

chevrons in single crochets
p. 54

raised chevrons
p. 99

chevrons and puff stitches
p. 100

rosettes
p. 102

simple ribbing
p. 95

ribbed half-double crochet
p. 49

raised scales
p. 107

ears of wheat
p. 132

lace fans
p. 142

Japanese fans
p. 126

closed garlands
p. 127

triangular leaves
p. 98

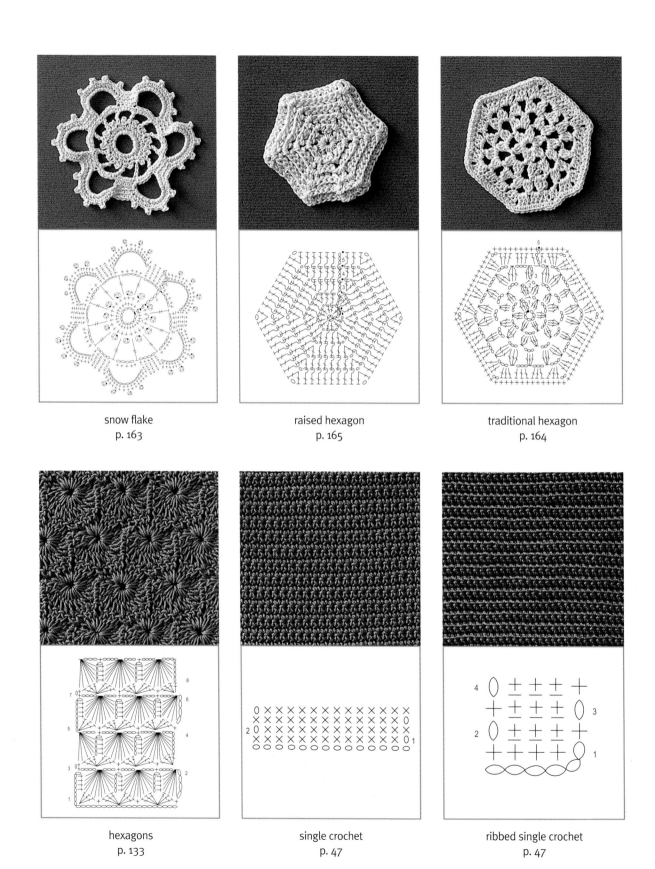

snow flake
p. 163

raised hexagon
p. 165

traditional hexagon
p. 164

hexagons
p. 133

single crochet
p. 47

ribbed single crochet
p. 47

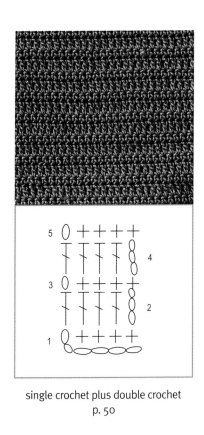

single crochet plus double crochet
p. 50

daisy
p. 170

Moorish medallion
p. 162

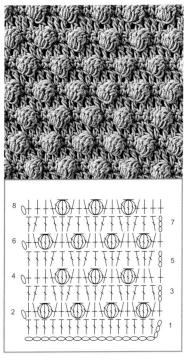

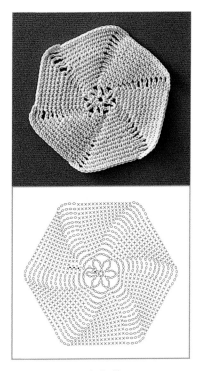

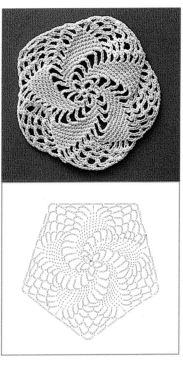

staggered cluster stitches
p. 104

windmill
p. 171

whirlpool
p. 172

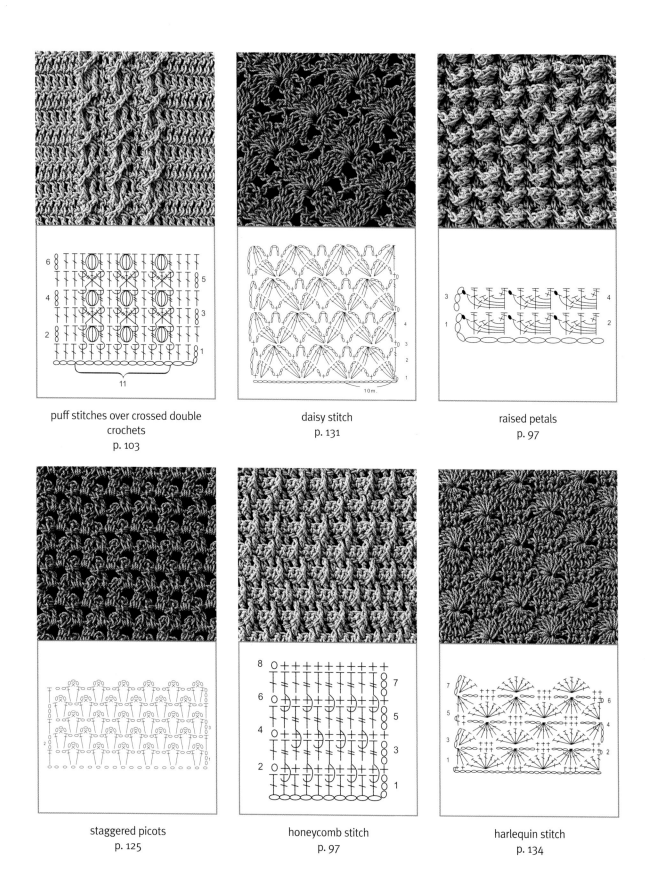

puff stitches over crossed double
crochets
p. 103

daisy stitch
p. 131

raised petals
p. 97

staggered picots
p. 125

honeycomb stitch
p. 97

harlequin stitch
p. 134

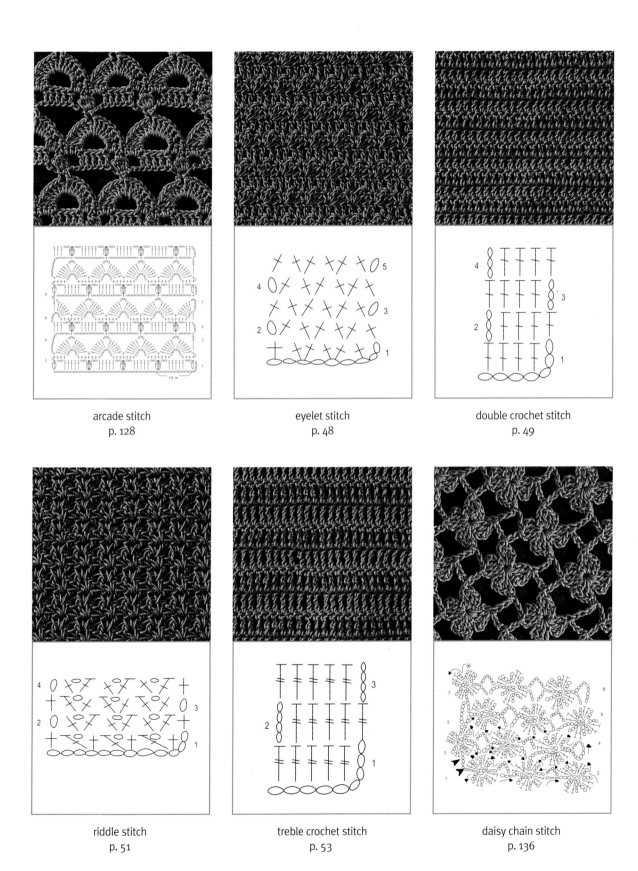

arcade stitch
p. 128

eyelet stitch
p. 48

double crochet stitch
p. 49

riddle stitch
p. 51

treble crochet stitch
p. 53

daisy chain stitch
p. 136

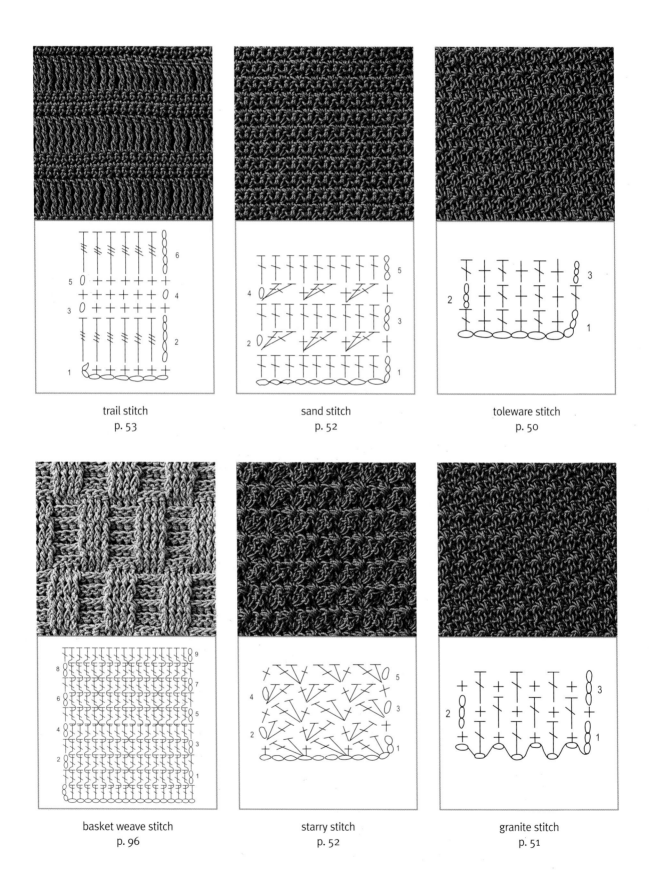

trail stitch
p. 53

sand stitch
p. 52

toleware stitch
p. 50

basket weave stitch
p. 96

starry stitch
p. 52

granite stitch
p. 51

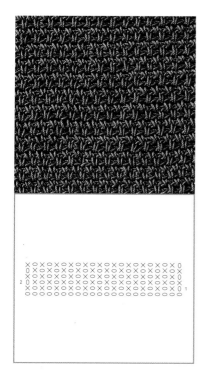

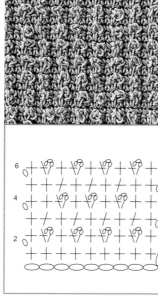

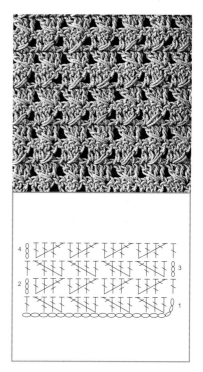

tight granite stitch
p. 48

granular stitch
p. 96

Mary quite contrary stitch
p. 106

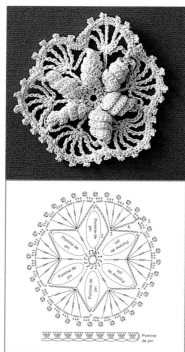

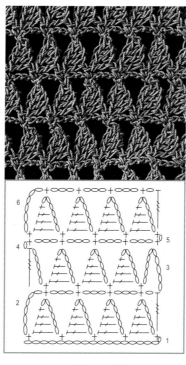

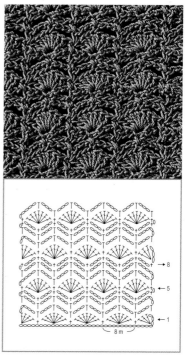

pine cones
p. 161

eyelet pyramids
p. 143

shell stripes stitch
p. 130

garland stripes
p. 135

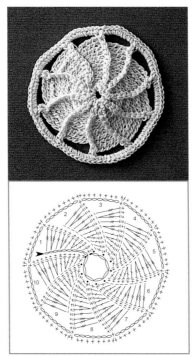

wheel
p. 174

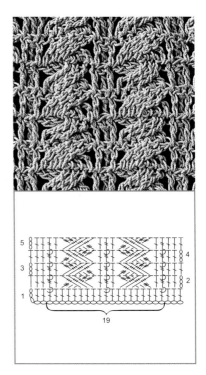

raised cables
p. 105

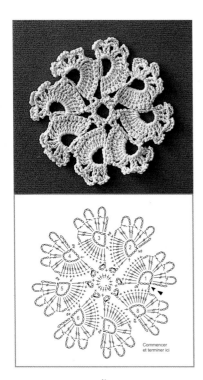

curlicue
p. 166

Techniques

Increase in the course of a row
p. 28

increase by 1 stitch at the
beginning of a row p. 26

increase by several stitches
at the end of a row p. 27

loop buttonhole
p. 35

horizontal buttonhole
p. 34

vertical buttonhole
p. 34

switch colors
p. 25

decrease by 1 stitch at the
end of a row p. 30

decrease by 1 stitch at the
beginning of a row p. 29

decrease by several dc
p. 31

decrease by several stitches at the
beginning of a row p. 30

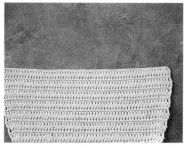

square armhole
p. 32

classic armhole
p. 32

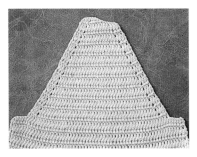

raglan armhole
p. 32

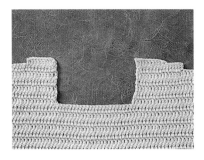

square neck
p. 33

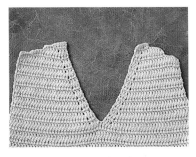

V neck
p. 33

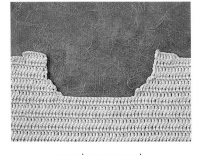

round or crew neck
p. 33

joining by needle with backstitch
p. 37

joining by overcasting with a needle
p. 37

joining with the crochet hook
p. 36

working in rows
p. 46

working in rounds
p. 160

Patterns in this book

Bucket bag
p. 56

Carry-all
p. 60

Baby pullover
p. 64

Cuddly toy
p. 68

Baby booties
p. 74

Jacket in ribbed single crochet
p. 80

Scarf and beret
p. 84

Square pillow
p. 108

Carrier bag
p. 111

Irish sweater
p. 114

Japanese pillow
p. 118

Shade trim
p. 144

Crib blanket
p. 145

Lacy scarf
p. 148

Slippers
p. 150

Tank top
p. 154

Accent pillow
p. 179

Lamp shade
p. 182

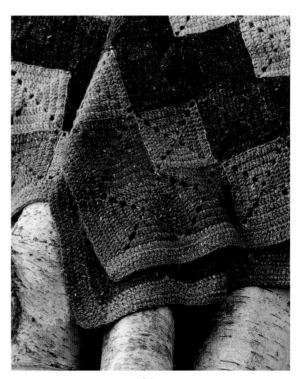

Afghan
p. 185

Brooches
p. 188

Belt
p. 190

Index

Jacket in Ribbed Single Crochet - cont. from page 82

FRONT BORDERS

Right: Rejoin the yarn with a sl st at right lower front with rs facing. Work 94 (100) sc down left front, ending at top of neck border.

Next row: Work sc to end.

Buttonholes: Next row work 4 sc, now * work (2 ch, skip 2 sts, 12 [13] sc), rep from * 6 times, end row by working 4 sc instead of 12 (13) sc.

Work straight in sc for 2 more rows. Fasten off.

Rejoin the yarn with a sl st at left neck with rs facing. Work 94 (100) sc down left front, and cont in sc for 4 rows. Fasten off.

Sew 7 buttons to the left front border opposite the buttonholes.

POCKETS (MAKE 2)

Work 20 ch sts for a base chain and cont with 14 rows of ribbed sc (st over st). Fasten off.

Border: Rejoin the yarn with a sl st on one side (not the base chain or fasten off edge) and work 22 sc to end of row. Cont with 4 rows of sc at right angles to the pocket ribbing. Fasten off.

Complete a second, identical pocket.

Using the darning or tapestry needle, slipstitch a pocket to each front 2-1/4 in (5.5 cm) from the base chain and 2 in (5 cm) from the side seam.

Sew a button at the centre of each pocket border.

Pattern instructions (cont.)

Irish sweater - cont. from page 116

Next row: Work forward with a sl st in the first st, pattern until 1 st remains; turn the work and pattern to end º.
Rep from º to º 3 times = 34 sts.
Cont straight in pattern for 1 (3) rows [end of Row 69 (75)].
Next row: Work forward with a sl st in the first st, pattern until 1 st remains; turn the work and pattern to end. Rep this row once.
Next row: Work forward with a sl st in each of the next 2 sts, pattern until 2 sts remain; turn the work and pattern to end.
Next row: Work forward with a sl st in each of the next 3 sts, pattern until 3 sts remain; turn the work and pattern to end = 20 sts.
Cont straight in pattern to the end of Row 82 (88). Fasten off,
Complete a second, identical sleeve.

ASSEMBLY

Darn in all the yarn ends.
Place front and back rs tog and backstitch the shoulder seams. Fit a shoulder cap into each armhole and backstitch the armhole, side, and sleeve seams.

NECKBAND
Rejoin the yarn with a sl st at the left shoulder seam and work 98 (102) sl sts around the neck, ending with a sl st over the first st of the rnd.
Rnd 1: 3 ch (= 1 dc), then work 1 dc over each sl st of the previous round.
Rnds 2–5: Follow the directions on p. 95 to complete these 4 rows in vertical ribbing (= 1-$\frac{1}{4}$ in [3 cm]). Fasten off.

Notes

Notes

Notes

Acknowledgments

To Anne-Laure Crozon and Aude Humbert of the Royal Paris/Coats Company.
To Auréa Polo for her valuable assistance.

Director: Jean-Louis Hocq
Editorial director: Suyapa Granda Bonilla
Editor: Sylvie Gauthier
Editorial assistant: Aline Flechel
Graphic design: Guylaine Moi
Layout: Laurence Ledru
Technical consultant: Renée Méri
Printing: APS
Charts: Reproscan
English Translation: Rosemary Perkins

Library of Congress Cataloging-in-Publication Data

Bayard, Marie-Noëlle, author.
[Crochet. English]
Crochet! : techniques, stitches, patterns / Marie-Noëlle Bayard ; Photography by Jean-Charles Vaillant ; English
Translation, Rosemary Perkins. -- First English Edition.
pages cm
Published originally under the title Le Crochet: Techniques et Modèles, copyright 2008 by Editions SOLAR, Paris.
Includes index.
ISBN 978-1-936096-14-5
1. Crocheting--Patterns. I. Vaillant, Jean-Charles. II. Perkins, Rosemary, translator. III. Title.
TT820.B3913 2011
746.43'4--dc22   2010044432

English translation ©: 2011 by Sixth & Spring Books
All rights reserved. No part of this publication may be reproduced or used in any form or by any means—graphic, electronic, or
mechanical, including photocopying, recording, or information storage-and-retrieval systems—without written permission of the
publisher. The written instructions, photographs, designs, projects and patterns are intended for the personal, noncommercial use of
the retail purchaser and are under federal copyright laws; they are not to be reproduced in any form for commercial use.

Manufactured in China
1 3 5 7 9 10 8 6 4 2
First English Edition